NEW TESTAMENT
EVERYDAY BIBLE STUDY SERIES

NEW TESTAMENT
EVERYDAY BIBLE STUDY SERIES

PHILIPPIANS AND
1 & 2 THESSALONIANS

SCOT MCKNIGHT

QUESTIONS WRITTEN BY
BECKY CASTLE MILLER

HarperChristian
Resources

*New Testament Everyday Bible Study Series: Philippians and
1, 2 Thessalonians*
© 2022 by Scot McKnight

Requests for information should be addressed to:
HarperChristian Resources, 3900 Sparks Dr. SE, Grand Rapids,
Michigan 49546

ISBN 978-0-310-12949-3 (softcover)
ISBN 978-0-310-12950-9 (ebook)

HarperChristian Resources titles may be purchased in bulk for church,
business, fundraising, or ministry use. For information, please e-mail
ResourceSpecialist@ChurchSource.com.

First Printing May 2022 / Printed in the United States of America

CONTENTS

1 THESSALONIANS

2 THESSALONIANS

For Lynn and Jim Cohick

GENERAL INTRODUCTION

Christians make a claim for the Bible not made of any other book. Or, since the Bible is a library shelf of many authors, it's a claim we make of no other shelf of books. We claim that God worked in each of the authors as they were writing so that what was scratched on papyrus expressed what God wanted communicated to the people of God. Which makes the New Testament a book unlike any other book. Which is why Christians are reading the NT almost two thousand years later with great delight. These books have the power to instruct us and to rebuke us and to correct us and to train us to walk with God every day. We read these books because God speaks to us in them.

Developing a routine of reading the Bible with an open heart, a receptive mind, and a flexible will is the why of the *New Testament Everyday Bible Studies*. But not every day will be the same. Some days we pause and take it in, and other days we stop and repent and lament and open ourselves to God's restoring graces. No one word suffices for what the Bible does to us. In fact, the Bible's view of the Bible can be found by reading Psalm 119, the longest chapter in the Bible with 176 verses! It is a meditation on eight terms for what the Bible is and what the Bible does to those who listen and read it. Its laws (*torah*) instruct us, its laws (*mishpat*) order us, its statutes direct us, its precepts inform us, its decrees guide us, its commands compel us, its words speak to us, and its promises comfort us, and it is no wonder that the author can sum all eight up as the "way" (119:3, 37). Each of those terms still speaks to what happens when we open our minds to the Word of God.

Every day with the Bible then is new because our timeless and timely God communes with us in our daily lives in our world and in our time. Just as God spoke to Jesus in Galilee and Paul in Ephesus and John on Patmos. These various contexts help us hear God in our context, so the *New Testament Everyday Bible Studies* will often delve into contexts.

Most of us now have a Bible on our devices. We may well have several translations available to us everywhere we go every day. To hear those words we are summoned by God to open the Bible, to attune our hearts to God, and to listen to what God says. My prayer is that these daily study guides will help each of us become daily Bible readers attentive to the mind of God.

PHILIPPIANS

INTRODUCTION: READING PAUL'S LETTER TO THE PHILIPPIANS

Philippians is one of the favorite letters of Paul for many Christians, not least because of its crisp ideas and special terms like joy and fellowship (a common life with others) and unity. Then too it has some of our favorite passages, like the poem of Philippians 2:6–11, and favorite verses, not least 4:13's "I can do all this through him who gives me strength." That Paul was in a tough situation, in prison in probably Rome, causes many to turn to this short letter for wisdom and comfort. He tells the Thessalonians that he "was treated outrageously in Philippi" itself (1 Thessalonians 2:2).

Philippi is a Roman colony, located between Thessalonica and today's Istanbul, and not far from the coast of the Aegean. It is a beautiful city and was proud of its Roman connection. Paul founded a church in Philippi, as recorded in Acts 16, which we can read about in the story of Lydia's conversion. Perhaps she has died and makes no appearance in this letter.

Most date this letter to Paul's time of imprisonment in Rome, thus about 60–63 AD, while others think he may have been in Ephesus, which would mean a date around

55 AD or so. We don't know for sure, though some make very strong statements of certainty. At least the expression "Caesar's household" in 4:22 sure does sound like someone in a Roman prison.

To read Philippians well I suggest reading it front to back several times and then read it slowly again, marking major themes and terms, like joy and common life. One of the more fascinating threads in this letter, and I encourage you to keep your eyes open for suggestions, is about financial support of Paul. There are lots of economic terms in this letter, especially in the last chapter, but the word often translated "fellowship" or "partnership," which we translate as "common life," has to do with this kind of generous sharing between them and Paul. Because this theme is not as easy to detect, I will begin the study guide with the most important passage on this theme, Philippians 4:10–20. Starting there changes how one reads the letter.

Overall, Paul writes an encouraging letter to the Philippians about his own life, about his confidence that he will be released, and about their value to him. Through the whole letter we sense the importance of a common life for the earliest Christians, and hence he urges them to think about this new way of life with one another. He wants them to learn humility in relating to one another.

Works cited in the Study Guide (throughout the Guide you will find the author's name and title as noted in this book listing with page numbers whenever I cite something from it):

Markus Bockmuehl, *A Commentary on the Epistle to the Philippians* (London: A&C Black, 1997). [Bockmuehl, *Philippians*]

Lynn Cohick, *Philippians,* Story of God Bible Commentary (Grand Rapids: Zondervan, 2013). [Cohick, *Philippians*]

James D.G. Dunn, *The Theology of Paul the Apostle* (Grand Rapids: Wm. B. Eerdmans, 1998). [Dunn, *Paul*]

Gordon D. Fee, *Paul's Letter to the Philippians* (Grand Rapids: Wm. B. Eerdmans, 1995). [Fee, *Philippians*]

G. Walter Hansen, *The Letter to the Philippians* (Grand Rapids: Wm. B. Eerdmans, 2009). [Hansen, *Philippians*]

Gerald F. Hawthorne, Ralph P. Martin, *Philippians* (rev. ed.; Grand Rapids: Zondervan, 2004). [Hawthorne, *Philippians*]

Scot McKnight, *Pastor Paul: Nurturing a Culture of Christoformity in the Church* (Grand Rapids: Brazos, 2019). [McKnight, *Paul*]

Carolyn Osiek, *Philippians and Philemon* (Nashville: Abingdon, 2000). [Osiek, *Philippians*]

Monya A. Stubbs, "Philippians," in Brian Blount, et al., *True to our Native Land: An African American New Testament Commentary* (Minneapolis: Fortress, 2007), 363–379. [Stubbs, *Philippians*]

N.T. Wright, *Paul and the Faithfulness of God* (Minneapolis: Fortress, 2013). [Wright, *Paul*]

A COMMON LIFE OF GRATITUDE FOR GENEROSITY

Philippians 4:10–20

Special Note to the Reader: We open this study guide to Philippians by starting with chapter 4:10–20 that sets the context before us. At the heart of Paul's letter is that he and they share a common life, and this passage puts into words major elements of that common life. Not the least of which is generosity with resources, which created a special bond with the Philippians and Paul and his co-workers. From this point on in the letter, every time we see the word "common life" or "fellowship" we need to have in mind the tangible, generous gifts at work in such a fellowship of believers.

[10] *I rejoiced greatly in the Lord that at last you renewed your concern for me. Indeed, you were concerned, but you had no opportunity to show it.* [11] *I am not saying this because I am in need, for I have learned to be content whatever the circumstances.* [12] *I know what it is to be in need, and I know what it is to have plenty. I have learned the secret of being content in any and every situation, whether well fed or hungry, whether living in plenty or in want.* [13] *I can do all this through him who gives me strength.*

14 Yet it was good of you to share in my troubles. 15 Moreover, as you Philippians know, in the early days of your acquaintance with the gospel, when I set out from Macedonia, not one church shared with me in the matter of giving and receiving, except you only; 16 for even when I was in Thessalonica, you sent me aid more than once when I was in need. 17 Not that I desire your gifts; what I desire is that more be credited to your account. 18 I have received full payment and have more than enough. I am amply supplied, now that I have received from Epaphroditus the gifts you sent. They are a fragrant offering, an acceptable sacrifice, pleasing to God. 19 And my God will meet all your needs according to the riches of his glory in Christ Jesus.

20 To our God and Father be glory for ever and ever. Amen.

The final passage in Philippians opens the front door to the entire letter because its theme shapes so much of this letter. It details Paul both being contented in all situations and thanking the Philippians for financially supporting him. A key word here gets translated with various English words but behind them all are *koinos*, which means "common," and *koinonia*, "common life" or "fellowship." But this common life is more than living a similar life. The terms indicate participating in one another's life and livelihood. It means praying for one another and supporting one another materially and participating with one another in a common mission. I have underlined the terms above where we see this.

Here's how Paul's understanding of common life of gratitude and generosity is constructed. First, God is a God of "grace," which is a similar term to "gift." Second, Jesus impoverished himself by becoming human and dying for our sins. This is the supreme act of God's giving or God's grace. Third, Jesus' intent in becoming poor was so that we could become rich through his grace and giving. Fourth, we receive his grace and so become rich in blessings so that, fifth, we can reciprocate in giving to others. By this *we participate in the cycle of God's generosity and grace*, the common life mentioned in this letter so often. Gift giving in the 1st Century created a social bond between giver and receiver, obligated the receiver to reciprocate in exchange, either by thanksgiving or more likely by a return gift, and this sealed their relationship (Barclay, *Paul and the Gift*). Our passage jumps right into this theory of generosity, not by explaining it but by doing it. Grace transforms humans into agents of grace. That's what happens with grace unleashed.

"Common life" in Philippians:

Phil. 1:5 because of your *partnership* in the gospel from the first day until now . . .

Phil. 1:7 It is right for me to feel this way about all of you, since I have you in my heart and, whether I am in chains or defending and confirming the gospel, all of you *share in* God's grace with me.

Phil. 2:1 Therefore if you have any encouragement from being united with Christ, if any comfort from his love, if any *common sharing* in the Spirit, if any tenderness and compassion,

Phil. 3:10 I want to know Christ—yes, to know the power of his resurrection and *participation* in his sufferings, becoming like him in his death,

> **Phil. 4:15** Moreover, as you Philippians know, in the early days of your acquaintance with the gospel, when I set out from Macedonia, not one church *shared with me* in the matter of giving and receiving, except you only.

But Paul seems to have had a common life policy about financial support that worked like this: he received no financial support as he was planting a church and when he resided in that church plant's city. Instead, while there, he worked a manual job to support himself and his co-workers. Once a church was on its own feet and probably in good order (unlike Corinth, from whom he seemed not to take funds) and Paul was on the road again, he would accept donations, that is, he and they could participate in a common life of generous giving and receiving. The Philippians would then have been mature enough to support him, and he welcomed their gifts. But this common life had some unusual twists and turns as it learned to express God's own gracious gift-giving. The best kind of common life involves gratitude, contentment, and affirmations.

GRATITUDE EXTENDED

The Philippians expressed their generosity to Paul in gift-giving of some sort, most likely in providing funds for his well-being and mission. This is seen in "you renewed your concern for me" (4:10) but at that time there was no opportunity for them to give. Instead, "it was good of you to share in my troubles" (4:14) but then he can say a gift has arrived through one of his best co-workers: "I have received full payment and have more than enough. I am amply supplied, now that I have received from Epaphroditus the gifts you sent" (4:18). The desire they had to help eventually led to a gift.

As believers who experience God's grace reciprocate in thanksgiving to God, so Paul expresses his gratitude in the above words. Noticeably he does not say "thanks" as one might expect. It's difficult to know why the word does not appear and perhaps too much has been made of its absence. It may be that Paul does not want to be drawn into a dependent relationship with them (Bockmuehl, *Philippians*, 256–258). Perhaps so, but I suggest Paul's understanding of grace and giving may well help us here. Christians know the gifts they receive from God lead to God's glory not to their having earned them. But Paul starts with giving the Philippians some glory, which is a kind of thanks. He says, "I desire . . . that more be credited to your account" (4:17). But he doesn't stop there as he extends that expression of gratitude to God when he says the gifts "are a fragrant offering, an acceptable sacrifice, *pleasing to God*" (4:18). He turns from them to giving God the glory. For Paul all thanks to others leads to a greater thanks and glory to God.

Christian responses to receiving gifts may well be expressed in a word of thanks to the givers but the ultimate glory belongs to God, not to the human giver. This should not shrink our expressions of thanks. Rather, this theory of generosity anchors all good gifts in God's good graces. Many of our churches and institutions have walls of honor for those who have given generously. May I recommend that at the bottom and the top of those names we say, "All for God's glory"?

Contentment Enlarged

Paul has received a gift from the Philippians, but he is at pains—read this aloud and you will feel the tension—to say they are not obligated to him and that he has learned the art of enlarged contentment, and "content" can be translated as "self-sufficient." Read 4:11–13 slowly. He's not "in need, for I have learned to be content," because he's learned to live "in plenty or in want." God is the one who gives him the strength to endure the "want" as he knows the goodness of generosity in times of "plenty." A few verses later he states this even more directly: "Not that I desire your gifts" (4:17). The word "desire" could be translated "seek after" or "push for."

There is no demand in Paul, and that means there is no sense of obligation or duty for the Philippians to respond to the gift of gospel grace preached to them by Paul. This counters one of the mostly unwritten rules of ancient gift giving. Receivers were to reciprocate as an obligation according to their own resources. Paul saws the legs off the table of obligation, and they discover they are sitting across from one another with nothing between them. They sit together as siblings who desire to be generous as an expression of gratitude to one another and to God. If they are unable at that time to provide for Paul, Paul's fine. If they are able, Paul's fine with that too.

We may need to work on the discipline of contentment more. That is, we (or I) live in an affluent Western world where we have all we need and far more. I can get irritated when my computer responds slower than I think it ought where Paul was learning to live without food and shelter and safety. Contentment is a Christian virtue that roots itself in God's providential care for us. Lenten disciplines remind us of our affluence as does sacrificial giving. Some of us serve the homeless or live among the poor and these too can remind us of our need for contentment.

AFFIRMATIONS EXPRESSED

The Philippians were early givers as we sometimes say in church talk after an appeal for funds. Way back "in the early days . . . not one church shared with me in the matter of giving and receiving," and we should notice his theory of generosity at work in "giving and receiving." Not one church "except you only" (4:15). They were then the early givers, and this surely gave Paul a sense of honor and pride in them. (Which they knew.) He is affirming them, and everyone in the church will hear this letter read aloud.

Public affirmations of givers can get dicey. Jesus had very strong words about giving in order to be seen (Matthew 6:1–4), and some will want to give in order to get public glory. True enough, but there is a Christian approach to publicly affirming givers. Paul's theory helps us. Let us learn to express thanksgiving to the wealthy givers among us through Paul's theory: God unleashed a kind of grace that transforms us into agents of grace, so our giving owes its energies in God's grace, and we are but agents who turn any gratitude into God's glory, not ours.

Not only does he affirm them, he also has a "back atcha" promise, something he has himself learned over the years in gospel work: "My God will meet all your needs according to the riches of his glory in Christ Jesus" (4:19). Again, this verse is a one-verse summary of 2 Corinthians 8–9. His theory is at work: God is a God of grace, God gives grace in Christ Jesus, we receive grace, we give thanks and glory to God, and we become agents of generosity because of that grace at work in us.

When he ties the knot on this section, he takes us to the goal of all his theory of generosity: God is to receive all the glory (4:20).

QUESTIONS FOR REFLECTION AND APPLICATION

1. What do Paul and the Philippians share with one another? What does their "common life" look like?

2. How does Christians' generosity to each other bring glory to God?

3. What seems to be Paul's policy about financial support from churches?

4. How can you cultivate contentedness in your life?

5. How would both your giving and your receiving gifts change if you embraced Paul's view that generosity glorifies God?

FOR FURTHER READING

John Barclay, *Paul and the Gift* (Grand Rapids: Wm. B. Eerdmans, 2015).

Charles Krauthammer, *The Point of it All: A Lifetime of Great Loves and Endeavors* (New York: Crown Forum, 2018), 177–178.

OUR COMMON LIFE

Philippians 1:1–11

¹ Paul and Timothy, servants of Christ Jesus,

To all God's holy people in Christ Jesus at Philippi, together with the overseers and deacons:

² Grace and peace to you from God our Father and the Lord Jesus Christ.

³ I thank my God every time I remember you. ⁴ In all my prayers for all of you, I always pray with joy ⁵ because of your partnership in the gospel from the first day until now, ⁶ being confident of this, that he who began a good work in you will carry it on to completion until the day of Christ Jesus.

⁷ It is right for me to feel this way about all of you, since I have you in my heart and, whether I am in chains or defending and confirming the gospel, all of you share in God's grace with me. ⁸ God can testify how I long for all of you with the affection of Christ Jesus.

⁹ And this is my prayer: that your love may abound more and more in knowledge and depth of insight, ¹⁰ so that you may be able to discern what is best and may be pure and blameless for the day of Christ, ¹¹ filled with the fruit of righteousness that comes through Jesus Christ—to the glory and praise of God.

Imagine two things as you read this passage. First, imagine the first two verses written on the front of an envelope. Those verses inform us of the sender and address as our envelopes do today. Second, imagine someone reading this letter aloud to the house churches in Philippi–in fact, not just reading but *performing* the letter in such a manner that you suddenly find yourself thinking you see Paul and Timothy and not the person standing there reading it. It is the reader's voice, but you hear Paul and Timothy. Timothy often occurs at the top of Paul's letters.* Not only are you hearing them, but you are feeling every word of the letter because the reader has so mastered the letter that he's (or she's) not even looking at it. She's (or he's) memorized it and you know the reader is even adlibbing at times to make it all very clear just for you. To imagine this, you and I will have to remove ourselves from thinking this is the Bible being read. We will have to remember this is an actual letter by actual authors sent and read to actual people in actual homes in the Roman colony Philippi, an utterly gorgeous colony not far from a decline down to the northern tip of the beautiful Aegean Sea.

Our Common Life

Paul and Timothy like the word "partnership," which can be translated as "fellowship" or "friendship" or "sharing" or "partnership" or "common life" or "together." The central idea is to participate with one another *in a common life*, which is a theme important to the entire letter. Lynn

---

* Notice 2 Corinthians 1:1; Colossians 1:1; 1 Thessalonians 1:1; 2 Thessalonians 1:1.

Cohick develops a linear thought process in this letter: God and our salvation in Christ leads to our life together in Christ (Cohick, *Philippians*, 1–2). There's that word "together." In this letter we have a common life "in the gospel" (1:5), in God's grace (1:7), in the Spirit (2:1), in the sufferings of Christ (3:10), in the troubles Paul himself experienced (4:14), and the need to share in one's provisions (4:15). It is indeed quite likely that the "partnership" of 1:5 also involved their providing financially for Paul's mission work (notice 2 Corinthians 9:15; see Bockmuehl, *Philippians*, 60). All of this is what life together looks like.

Our Greetings

Believers in Jesus can greet one another in ways they can't greet others. Notice how the authors identify themselves: "servants of Christ Jesus." Actually the word is stronger so it's worth running a line through your word "servant" and writing "slaves" above it. To call themselves slaves both locates them at the bottom of the status heap and affirms the intensity of their devotion to the Lord Jesus (see 1 Corinthians 6:20). Oddly enough, in this common life to be a slave of Christ is to be at the top of the status heap. We will soon read that Jesus himself was a slave (Philippians 2:7)! Plus, some of God's major leaders in the Bible used the term "slave" for themselves. (Moses: Numbers 12:7; Prophets: Jeremiah 25:4). With one another we know our relationship to Jesus: he is Lord, and we are but slaves of the Lord. Carolyn Osiek makes an important observation: "A slave's status did not derive from the legal condition of slavery, but from the status of his or her owner, the slave's own position, and its importance"

(Osiek, *Philippians*, 34). For a Christian to be a slave of Jesus was to be owned by the Lord of all, and this would have given the Christian transcendent status. Lynn Cohick rightly counters the leadership craze of our culture with the terms Paul and Timothy use for themselves. They are not "leaders" or "vision casters" or "entrepreneurs" or "senior pastors" or "teaching pastors" but slaves together of the Lord Jesus (Cohick, *Philippians*, 26–32).

They address their letter to "all," not just the upper crust and inner wheels, "God's holy people." This does not mean these people are sinless, because the term "holy" means someone devoted to God and therefore no longer devoted to Rome and its gods, to the market and its monies, or to status growth in the Roman upward climb to honor and fame and glory and a monument on Main Street when you die. His wish for them is to know and to indwell in the special "grace and peace" that come our way only in the power of God the Father and in the "Lord Jesus Christ." There's some definite insider talk, but it all is set up for a major theme in this letter: fellowship or the common life together that believers in Jesus now have in Philippi.

OUR AFFECTIONS

The common life of Christians means reciprocating affections for one another. So many think of Paul as some gruff old guy hobbling along, always in a hurry, from city to city along the Mediterranean barking out orders to one new church after another. Any reading of Philippians 1:7–8 reveals to the contrary a warm and fuzzy Paul! He says they hold him in his heart, like our saying "I heart you!," and they together share in God's abundant grace of redemption and love and transformation. They risk this new life together even though he is in prison in Rome for gospeling, and we might need to learn again that identifying with an imprisoned troublemaker does not make for friends with Philippi's Rome-based authorities. In fact, they share a life in preaching the gospel. All this is in verse seven.

Then Paul goes fizzy in his fuzzy: "I long for all of you with the compassion of Christ Jesus" (1:8). His love for them is the kind of love that lays down one's life for others. He learned the heart of a life together in the way Jesus lived (and we'll see more of this in chapter two). A common life entails affections in our relationships with one another, but this common life is more than the classical sense of friendship because (1) it is in Christ and (2) it transcends gender and status. Friendship in the Roman world was voluntary, between males especially, and was elitist. Paul never calls another believer "friend" because their relationship is deeper than friendship; they are siblings (McKnight, *Pastor Paul*, 31–78).

OUR PRAYERS

Since Paul speaks so much in the first person ("I" and "me" and "my") we need to remind ourselves that Timothy was a co-author and not just a co-sender (1:1). After all, Timothy's not just sitting there letting Paul make all the decisions. The letter is Paul's voice but behind that voice were contributions from Timothy. The Philippians knew Timothy well: he was with Paul when the church was planted (Acts 16:3–4), and Paul is about to send Timothy to Philippi (Philippians 2:19–23).

A common life in Christ includes praying for one another. We discover the theme of prayer in 1:3–6 and 1:9–11. It's not hard to exaggerate verse three: "I thank my God every time I remember you" can make us think Paul was thanking God for them every day all day long, but behind his "every time" is the common spiritual practice of praying what we today call the "hours of prayer." That is, Jews prayed at sunset, at sunrise, and in the middle of the day. Three times a day. Every day. Except on the day of the funeral of one's parents. Three times a day Paul says he prayed for the Philippians. He prays "with joy." When this was read to the churches in Philippi there were some smiles of pride about Paul's affirmations. His joyful prayers are rooted in their common life commitment to the work of the gospel–preaching it and teaching it and living it and suffering for it–and his utter confidence in God's powerful work of transforming the Philippian believers into people fit for the eternal presence of God. In spite of appearances, the work of God cannot be stopped.

We can learn how to pray for others in following the categories Paul uses for his intercessions for the Philippian believers. His prayers were not reducible to the "Bless Sarah and Sam" prayers we so often hear. No, he prayed specifically for profound transformations (1:9–11). As the Lord's Prayer can be a model prayer for us, so this prayer can be a guide for all those ministering, mentoring, and parenting others.

First, he prays for their love to flourish (1:9). To "flourish" is not so much bigger and better as it is deeper and wider.

Second, he prays their love will flourish into "knowledge and depth of insight," that is, into wise living (1:9). This flips the order for moderns who think first comes knowledge then comes love. Not so for Paul: love leads to a deeper knowing. N.T. Wright has often observed this order: "Ordinary human wisdom, ordinary human knowledge, is not just cancelled. It is taken up into something" and that "new 'something' is *agape*, love" (Wright, *Paul and the Faithfulness of God*, 1356).

Third, he prays their flourishing wise love will lead to profound discernment of how to live as believers in Philippi (1:10).

And fourth, following hard on this flourishing, wise, and discerning love, that the vines of their moral life will be loaded with the fruit of doing what is right–a kind of doing that can only be accomplished because of their common life participation in Christ (1:11). Notice how Paul's petitions unfold:

Love
Flourishing
Wisdom
Discernment
Right-living
God's glory!

Such an orderly unfolding set of prayers leads me to examine what I pray for when I pray for others. One leads to the next and the next and so on until it brings "glory and praise" to God, not to the believers, not to Paul and Timothy, and not to the "overseers and deacons" (1:1), that is, supervisors (or mentors) and servants. That they single out these leaders cracks a door slightly on church order and pastoral care in Philippi and the importance they will have in explaining the letter.

A common life will include our greetings, our affections, and our prayers. And next we will see it involves mission.

Questions for Reflection and Application

1. What are some key elements of the "common life" together in Christian living as seen in Philippians?

2. How does Paul and Timothy calling themselves "slaves" run counter to today's culture of church leadership?

3. What are the elements of Paul's prayers for the Philippians?

4. Think about your relationships. Who in your Christian life has been to you like Timothy to Paul? Like Paul to Timothy? Like the Philippians to Paul, and vice versa?

5. Write a prayer for a beloved Christian friend or church community following Paul's prayer model.

A COMMON LIFE IN THE GOSPEL MISSION

Philippians 1:12–26

12 Now I want you to know, brothers and sisters, that what has happened to me has actually served to advance the gospel. 13 As a result, it has become clear throughout the whole palace guard and to everyone else that I am in chains for Christ. 14 And because of my chains, most of the brothers and sisters have become confident in the Lord and dare all the more to proclaim the gospel without fear.

15 It is true that some preach Christ out of envy and rivalry, but others out of goodwill. 16 The latter do so out of love, knowing that I am put here for the defense of the gospel. 17 The former preach Christ out of selfish ambition, not sincerely, supposing that they can stir up trouble for me while I am in chains. 18 But what does it matter? The important thing is that in every way, whether from false motives or true, Christ is preached. And because of this I rejoice. Yes, and I will continue to rejoice, 19 for I know that through your prayers and God's provision of the Spirit of Jesus Christ what has happened to me will turn out for my deliverance. 20 I eagerly expect and hope that I will in no way be ashamed, but will have sufficient courage so that now as always Christ will be exalted in my body, whether by life or by death. [21] For to me, to live is Christ and to die is gain. [22] If I am to go on living in the body, this will mean fruitful labor for me. Yet what shall I choose? I do not know! [23] I am torn between the two: I desire to depart and be with Christ, which is better by far; [24] but it is more necessary for you that I remain in the body. [25] Convinced of this, I know that I will remain, and I will continue with all of you for your progress and joy in the faith, [26] so that through my being with you again your boasting in Christ Jesus will abound on account of me.

Pressure applied to a person, whether physical or emotional or financial, often reveals character. Persecution, whether physical or social and status-shaming, puts a person in the dock to declare (or not) her allegiance to Jesus as the world's true Lord and King. Instead of blaming others, instead of running to safety, and instead of going silent, the faithful believer confesses before her persecutors and says, "Jesus is the Lord. He is my Lord. And I will follow him." Paul knew pressure. In fact, it is more than possible he had been in prison for four years (two in Caesarea, two in Rome). But, instead of pouting and moaning, he responded with bold confessions of the Lord Jesus. Remember back when Paul was first in Philippi? You might know the impact of that singular witness by Paul in prison. We call the impact the "Philippian Jailer," as we read about him in Acts 16.

Pressure also reveals personality, and this passage is special among the Pauline letters for all its I's and Me's and My's. (You might underline each one in the passage above.) However, he is not being self-centered. Rather, Paul lives in an honor-shame world where everyone knew their status location in society. Being in prison for being connected to a crucified Galilean man degraded one's status. But Paul flipped the honor-shame script: what was degrading for the Romans was for Paul upgrading or honoring, and what was honoring among the Romans was degrading for the apostle (Osiek, *Philippians*, 45–47). The whole letter in some ways turns on this flipped script. Paul's "I" is actually "Christ."

WE NEED COURAGE

Paul is sitting in prison where he awaits a trial and verdict. One was not sent to prison *after* but *before* one's sentence in that world. One was in prison to await trial. We see this in Paul's own life while in Caesarea Maritima (Acts 23–26). Paul experiences an entirely new perspective on sufferings that promotes his courage. He perceives that his imprisonment enabled him to "advance the gospel" (Philippians 1:12). How so? "It has become clear" or even "obvious" to the entire Roman Praetorian Guard, a massive group of soldiers who protected no less than the emperor (Nero), that his imprisonment is because of his witness "for Christ" (1:13). He'd done nothing other than tell people that Jesus is the Lord. Paul turned his imprisonment in Philippi in his original mission there into an opportunity to gospel the inmates and authorities (Acts 16:19–34). He was doing the same thing again in Rome. It was the Pauline prison habit.

Paul and Timothy knew the reality of opposition to the gospel, which meant the sting of rejection, the shame of verbal insults, and the wounds of persecutions. His witness in prison in Rome has made others "confident in the Lord" so that they "dare all the more" to tell others about the Lordship of Jesus (Philippians 1:14). One suspects Paul is urging the Philippians to learn from this description of his own experience, and that is why he describes them inclusively as "brothers and sisters" or siblings (1:12). In the next passage he makes their common experience explicit: "since you are going through the same struggle you saw I had" (1:30; Fee, *Philippians*, 107).

Sibling language evokes equality and that we are all in this together. People are watching us. Our children absorb the patterns of our lives, our neighbors observe us, our workmates notice us, our church scans us, and the community watches our witness. Our fellow believers are en*couraged* by our courage and em*powered* by the power at work in us. They see that we don't lash out but that we absorb opposition to the gospel as we walk in the way of the cross of Jesus. They notice that our rejections look like rejections of Christ.

WE KNOW OUR MESSAGE

In all that experience of suffering only one thing mattered: "Christ is preached" (1:18). In a few of his letters Paul clarifies what "gospel" means. First Corinthians 15:1–8 is the classic example, but so too one should read both Romans 1:2–4 and 2 Timothy 2:8. The essence of the gospel is the story about Jesus that fulfills the promises of Israel's story, and this Jesus is announced in the gospel. Correct that: announcing and talking about Jesus is gospeling! This Jesus is the King, the Messiah, the Lord, and the Savior, and as Savior he brings all the benefits of salvation (forgiveness, justification, reconciliation, transformation; McKnight, *King Jesus Gospel*). Paul is in prison because of his "defense of the gospel," that is, for what he was gospeling about Jesus (1:16).

As one who cares about Christian orthodoxy and faithfulness to the faith I can get a little anxious when Paul says that "some preaching Christ" do so in a quest for glory and honor (1:15) or they do so out of "selfish ambition" (1:17). Are they, I ask, truly preaching Christ? Anyone watching the current American church scene knows this happens. Sadly, some are inadvertently preaching the gospel as they tear apart the reputation of Paul (1:17).

It takes a big-hearted person to say, "Hey, they may not like me. They may oppose me. But they are at least telling people about Jesus!" Which is exactly what Paul says (1:18), and he who said this is one who wrote stinging words against those who were preaching a false gospel. In chapter three he will call false gospelers "dogs" and "evil workers" and "those who mutilate the flesh" (3:2 ESV). Strong disagreements to be sure! It's hard to square up all these words.

When I scan the shelves of bookstores or read widely today on internet web pages and blogs, I observe wildly different messages. There are conservatives and progressives, both utterly convinced of their rectitude. There are Calvinists and Arminians and Baptists and Anglicans. When I read Philippians 1:18 and mutter Paul's question to myself, which was "But does it matter?" and know his answer is "Christ is preached," I ask if my heart is big enough to stand with Paul. How about you? Sure, let's cut this down in size to say, "What is claimed by others in the name of Christ still has to be consistent with the gospel." Sure, I'll sing harmony (or, I'll at least try) with you on that one. But most of what we fight about on the internet is not whether or not we agree with Jesus being the North

Star but what in many ways is peripheral and, to be frank, *does not even matter.*

What I return to in reading this passage is one simple observation: *let's concentrate our hearts and minds and souls on Jesus as the Lord and let everything be subsumed to that message.* For some this sounds trite. I disagree. It is one of the greatest challenges of anyone preaching or teaching or leading to constrain what is said and done to what gives glory to Jesus.

WE CAN HAVE JOY

The word "joy" (or "rejoice") has a habit of showing up in the New Testament when suffering and persecution also show up.* You say "Persecution" and the early Christians cheer back with "Rejoice!" But theirs was not some kind of stoical endurance or some positive trick of the mind or some soul over body theory. Theirs was a fully embodied, emotional joy for the opportunity to walk with Jesus in the way of the cross. Tom Holland (not the actor), in his magisterial romp through the history of how the modern world became more Christian than often recognized, in one chapter zeroed in on Lyons (in Gaul) in the days of Irenaeus. Of the Christians suffering persecution then he writes, "Whether gored by bulls, or savaged by dogs, or roasted on red-hot chairs of iron, they cried out only 'the words they had repeated all along–the declarations of their faith'" (Holland, *Dominion*, 110). You say "Persecution" and they rejoice in the power of the resurrection. They could say this because they knew Jesus was with them, and

---

* Notice 2 Corinthians 8:2; Colossians 1:11; 1 Thessalonians 1:6; Hebrews 10:34; 12:2, 11; James 1:2; 1 Peter 1:8.

they knew they were suffering with him. Amazingly they found joy in the midst of suffering.

His theme of joy hears another tone. The Philippians participate in his release from prison by their prayers (1:19). Even deeper than that, his joy and confidence are rooted in "God's provision of the Spirit of Jesus Christ." I like to point out that "provision" can be translated "orchestration" (Greek *epichorēgia*). The Philippians were praying, but the Spirit will orchestrate the release and more ("my deliverance"). Confidence in that invisible orchestration gave them joy, which means this joy is a confidence in the irresistible work of God. His expression "will turn out for my deliverance" echoes the words of Job (13:16; Bockmuehl, *Philippians*, 82–83) and "deliverance" evokes not only release from prison but ultimate vindication by God.

WE LIVE IN HOPE

Christian hope is not simplistic "I hope so." Hope is not so much utter certainty as it is confidence in the God who promises. Sufficient experiences have made Paul confidently hopeful of deliverance (1:25–26; 2:24). Perhaps his most confident claim of hope is to be found near the end of his life in 2 Timothy 4:18 where, in prison again, he says "The Lord will rescue me from every evil attack and save me for his heavenly kingdom." The translation in Philippians 1:20, "I eagerly expect," is a little more precise than the original, which could be translated "according to [or consistent with] my eager expectation and my hope." These two terms–expectation and hope–express the courage necessary for him to remain faithful in the face of persecution. He is so confident in his hope that he knows he will "in no way be ashamed" (1:20). That is, God will vindicate those faithful to the gospel, either in this life or in the next.

Whether he dies into the presence of God or survives, he just wants "Christ to be exalted in my body" (1:20). This is an amazing expression. He wants his *body* to glorify God because it is in the *body* that he hopes and witnesses to Christ. One of his most famous lines follows: "to live is Christ and to die is gain" (1:21). Gerald Hawthorne tells us that Paul here lets us in on "the turmoil of his soul" (Hawthorne, *Philippians*, 64), which the NIV in 1:23 translates as "torn between the two" options: if he does not survive the emperor's judgment he will be with Christ; if he does, he will tell the world about Christ. Either way, it is all about Christ! Noticeably, so much was he aching to be with Christ–for him to see Jesus again–that he wasn't sure which he wanted: death or life.

So he intuits–and I don't know how else to explain his next words–that "I will remain" (1:25), that is, live on to minister the gospel so they can "progress" into Christlikeness. A wonderful image is used with this term "progress": the term means "cut one's way through something one hack at a time." That image is tied to "joy" and both are formed "in the faith." Paul seems to give himself quite the credit here for that progress. He says, "through my being with you again" and "on account of me" you Philippians will be boasting *in Christ*. The overall aim though gets it just right: Paul gets no credit. It all goes to Christ, but he does realize the importance of his giftedness and ministry at this time in their hacking way forward in Christian growth.

QUESTIONS FOR REFLECTION
AND APPLICATION

1. Hope and joy in this passage are more than simply spiritual states—they are real emotions. What role do joy and hope play in Paul's life?

2. Paul turns shame into honor and prison into a gospel mission. How do you think Paul accomplished turning things upside down in his culture?

3. What is the gospel, according to McKnight?

4. Is your heart big enough to stand with Paul to say about those opposing you or those seeking selfish fame, "at least they are preaching Christ"? If not, what would it take for God to work that out in your heart?

5. How do true, emotional hope and joy function in your life in Christ?

FOR FURTHER READING

Tom Holland, *Dominion: How the Christian Revolution Remade the World* (New York: Basic Books, 2019).

Scot McKnight, *The King Jesus Gospel: The Original Good News Revisited*, 2d. ed. (Grand Rapids: Zondervan, 2015).

A COMMON LIFE
OF SUFFERING

Philippians 1:27–30

²⁷ Whatever happens, conduct yourselves in a manner worthy of the gospel of Christ. Then, whether I come and see you or only hear about you in my absence, I will know that you stand firm in the one Spirit, striving together as one for the faith of the gospel ²⁸ without being frightened in any way by those who oppose you. This is a sign to them that they will be destroyed, but that you will be saved—and that by God. ²⁹ For it has been granted to you on behalf of Christ not only to believe in him, but also to suffer for him, ³⁰ since you are going through the same struggle you saw I had, and now hear that I still have.

How do some people seem to be prepared to endure suffering for Christ? When I was a child, our church celebrated global missions with an annual conference. Every year we heard about someone suffering for the gospel. The stories were not only uplifting but challenging. *Would I be willing to endure the same?* I sometimes asked myself. I also heard stories from *Foxe's Book of Martyrs*, which put suffering on the top tier of Christian experiences. As a college student I learned the stories of Dietrich Bonhoeffer under Hitler and Nelson Mandela under South African apartheid. Some are prepared because they have learned such stories and have witnessed suffering for the gospel. Suffering for Jesus was the way of the church in the earliest decades (and centuries).

Paul's persecution stories were known to the Philippians. But Paul's instructions transcend storytelling, and his instructions are all formed into one very long sentence—yes, 1:27–30 is one sentence in Greek. In fact, as Carolyn Osiek observes, this long sentence forms the core message of the entire letter (Osiek, *Philippians*, 47). The message is that the Christian life is a "public act having social or community consequences" (Cohick, *Philippians*, 70), including opposition that may lead to extreme consequences.

First, he begins at the beginning of all Christian living: *become a King Jesus citizen*. The NIV's "conduct yourselves" translates the Greek word *politeuomai*, and if you stare at it, you can see it stands behind our word "politics." My friend and colleague, Nijay Gupta, paraphrases it so well with "be good citizens of the gospel kingdom of Christ." Such a claim to a King Jesus citizenship demoted a claim to Roman citizenship. Gupta describes what Paul meant with these claims:

1. The earth may be our home, but our commonwealth is heaven (3:20).
2. Our enemy is not the state or a party but sin.
3. We are called to be a light together.
4. And this heavenly commonwealth has higher standards for our behavior (Gupta).

Bockmuehl describes it as a lifestyle that "is conceived as a deliberate, publicly visible, and . . . *politically* relevant" way of life (Bockmuehl, *Philippians*, 97). A kingdom worldview prepares a person to endure hardship for the kingdom, and that's exactly what "worthy of the gospel of Christ" means.

Second, we are empowered to be kingdom citizens when we "stand firm in the one Spirit" (1:27). Now that's a stunning expression. You may know that the Greek word for "Spirit" is *pneuma*, which can be translated as wind. Every Christmas season folks in our community have Santas and Angels and Elves that lay flat during the day but are filled with air in the evening. And they have lights. Paul's image works similarly: the Spirit fills us up so much we can stand up for Christ as citizens of King Jesus. The "one" Spirit is the Spirit that brings us into a common life, a united front in a divided world.

Third, the image behind "striving together" suggests athletes training or competing *with one another* to achieve victory (1:27; notice the same term at 4:3). Instead of training for a laurel wreath, the Roman world's gold medal, they are training in faithful allegiance to the gospel and its reward of the kingdom. Training like this produces fearless courage to live under King Jesus (1:28).

A fourth element of their readiness to face whatever comes their way is a famous Christian irony. We find it in 1:28. The experience of faithful endurance to opposition reveals its exact opposite, namely, that their opponents will meet God in judgment but the Philippian faithful "will be saved"! This element's irony is underscored when Paul says in 1:29–30 that suffering is a gift from God because in suffering they join Paul who joins Jesus. Nothing was more Christian for those first believers than participating in the sufferings Christ himself suffered. It is not clear who these opponents are. However, that Paul connects their suffering to his could indicate they too are experiencing harassment from the Roman authorities. It must be stated as well, perhaps because we are insensitive at this point, that Paul is not endorsing suffering as redemptive. As Monya Stubbs puts it, Paul here "does not sacralize suffering" (Stubbs, *Philippians*, 370). No, rather, this suffering is the result of joining in what God is doing and experiencing the backhand of evil and injustice–all in a struggle to bring about God's justice.

QUESTIONS FOR REFLECTION AND APPLICATION

1. What is the core message of Philippians, summarized in this section of the letter?

2. What does it mean to be a good citizen of God's kingdom, according to Nijay Gupta?

3. How does the Holy Spirit empower our Godly citizenship?

4. How does Paul connect the suffering of faithful followers with the suffering of Jesus?

5. How well prepared are you to endure suffering for Jesus? What could you do to become better prepared?

FOR FURTHER READING

Nijay Gupta, "Living as Good Citizens of the Gospel Kingdom of Christ according to Philippians," in Nijay Gupta, Tara Beth Leach, Matthew W. Bates, and Drew J. Strait, *Living the King Jesus Gospel: Discipleship and Ministry Then and Now* (Eugene, Oregon: Cascade, 2021), 65–79.

A COMMON LIFE
EXAMPLES

Philippians 2:1–4

¹ Therefore
>*if you have any encouragement from being united with Christ,*
>*if any comfort from his love,*
>*if any common sharing in the Spirit,*
>*if any tenderness and compassion,*
>*² then make my joy complete by being*
>*like-minded,*
>*having the same love,*
>*being one in spirit and*
>*of one mind.*
>*³ Do nothing out of selfish ambition or vain conceit. Rather,*
in humility value others above yourselves, ⁴ not looking to your
own interests but each of you to the interests of the others.

Living in unity as a fellowship, or a common life together, is a great idea. *Until you have to get along with someone you don't like.* It only takes a little while to encounter such a person. We cannot expect uniformity or consensus on everything, but we are to strive for an achievable unity.

The emphasis on a common life and unity in this short letter requires that we assume fractures and fissures had formed among the believers in Philippi, and Paul is urging them to transcend their divisions.

The apostle proposes in our verses a theological basis that appeals to the "affective faculties" (Osiek, *Philippians*, 52). Just as Philippians 1:27–30 was one long sentence, so 2:1–4 is another one and a rather complex one at that. Verse one is the *If-clause* and verses two through four are the *then-clause*: This "if" could be translated "since" or "supposing" or "assuming." That is, *assuming* verse one to be the case, verses two through four should happen! That is, if you've got all these blessings then you can also achieve unity with one another. The translation above is reformatted to make the listing more visible.

IF . . .

Notice that there are four terms here in verse one—"encouragement," "comfort," "common sharing," and the doubled expression "tenderness and compassion." The "encouragement" and "comfort" result "from being united with Christ," and the "common sharing" or fellowship, along with "tenderness and compassion," derive from "the Spirit." We can diagram it like this:

> Encouragement and comfort **in Christ** (2:1a).
> Common life, tenderness and compassion **in the Spirit** (2:1b).

Verse one then describes what we get from God (87), that is, these items are God-given, emotionally experienced redemptive realities. They are not human virtues. They are palpable intimacies we feel in our relationship with Christ and the Spirit. Cohick observes that "The church's life force is the breath of the Spirit, the blood of Jesus, the mind of Christ, the will of the Father" (Cohick, *Philippians*, 89).

Let me then just jump ahead to get right to the point: *If God is at work in you in Christ and in the Spirit, you can grow as well to experience unity's virtues.* The blessings of verse one, then, are not hard-earned moral accomplishments. They are instead grace-empowered, Christ-achieved, and Spirit-drenched acts of God in us.

. . . THEN

If God is at work in you, Paul says, *Make me happy!* That is, "make my joy compete" or "fill me up with joy." What makes Paul happy? Let's broaden that: What makes the Christian discipler, the pastor, the mentor, the parent, the teacher happy? God-established unities. Paul lists four of these unities in 2:2–the "like-minded," the "same love," "one in spirit," and "one mind." Monya Stubbs puts it all into a three-word package: "communal mental cohesiveness" (Stubbs, "Philippians," 370).

Before we move on, a brief clarification. The NIV's "one in spirit" surely misleads as much as it helps. The Greek expression, literally, is something like "co-souled" or "one-souled" or "together in soul." It combines the term for *with* and the term *psyche*, which is often translated "soul." The normal word for "spirit" or "Spirit" is not here. What Paul wrote says it all: he wants them to be co-souled, or together at the core of their very being, together in life's basic principle for living.

But unity is not uniformity. We are not going to get everyone on the same page about the same concerns. We can't get people to agree on songs or lengths of sermons or women preaching or the rapture or war or racial reconciliation or financial equities. The Bible's not creating a dream world. It knows we don't agree and wants us to strive for unity *in the midst of differences*. I can worship with someone who is either Democrat or Republican because unity in Christ transcends partisan politics.

The one-nesses in verse two are God-formed participations in Christ and the Spirit that yield capacities to live with one another's differences in behaviors and attitudes and feelings. But this unity transcends differences. Yes, something needs to be heard because we easily miss it. Paul's emphasis on equality and sameness horrified those intoxicated with the Roman system of upward mobility (Cohick, *Philippians*, 90). A God-shaped unity empowers the believers to shed "selfish ambition" and "vain conceit" (or airheadedness), two habits of life that flourished in the lives of those committed to the ways of Rome. Bockmuehl cleverly describes them as "that strangely addictive and debasing cocktail of vanity and public opinion" (Bockmuehl, *Philippians*, 110).

The Christian solution is so un-Roman but it is just as un-American. God calls us to "humility," a Christian virtue that turns the way of Rome upside down into valuing others above oneself. In that world humility was the same as humiliation (Cohick, *Philippians*, 93). A Christlike and Spirit-given life opens up for us a way of life that turns away from our "own interests" to favor "the interests of others." Paul speaks here into the world of vain-seeking glory in the public sector. He is not criticizing the need for a healthy self-image or denying the sacred importance of emotional, psychological boundaries. Tension between boundaries to protect ourselves and actions for the sake of others accompanies all genuine Christian living. Respecting the boundaries others have for themselves reflects what "the interests of others" actually means.

You may know what comes next in Philippians, and it is best to put this book down now to read Philippians 2:1–11 straight through. We are done now with 2:1–4 and Paul is about to write up an early Christian song about Jesus that becomes the paradigm of paradigms for how the Philippians were to live with one another in a most *un*-Roman of ways! The selfish tendencies of a Philippian life is challenged by the Christlike life, all visibly embodied in the life of Jesus (2:5–11). Think about it this way: kingdom citizens (1:27–30) who are led by Christ in the Spirit (2:1) can achieve a unity (2:2) by living like Christ (2:5–11), that is, denying self-interest and thinking of the others (2:3–4).

Easier said than done.

QUESTIONS FOR REFLECTION AND APPLICATION

1. How does the Holy Spirit work in us to generate fellowship and community?

2. What is the difference between unity and uniformity in the church?

3. What has been your experience with church unity, or church disunity? How have those experiences impacted you?

4. How is humility un-Roman and un-American?

5. McKnight writes about the tension between our boundaries to protect ourselves and the actions we take on behalf of others. How do you balance caring for yourself in healthy ways with also living a life of service to others?

THE COMMON LIFE OF GOD

Philippians 2:5–11

⁵ *In your relationships with one another, have the*
same mindset as Christ Jesus:
⁶ *Who, being in very nature God,*
did not consider equality with God something to
be used to his own advantage;
⁷ *rather, he made himself nothing*
by taking the very nature of a servant,
being made in human likeness.
⁸ *And being found in appearance as a man,*
he humbled himself
by becoming obedient to death—
even death on a cross!
⁹ *Therefore God exalted him to the highest place*
and gave him the name that is above every name,
¹⁰ *that at the name of Jesus every knee should*
bow,
in heaven and on earth and under the earth,
¹¹ *and every tongue acknowledge that Jesus Christ*
is Lord,
to the glory of God the Father.

The common life into which Christians are to grow transcends the business strategy of building a cohesive team, to get along with others in the city of Philippi, or to be effective in ministry. Each may be desirable but there is something profoundly deep about the common life into which Christians are to be formed. What is said in Philippians 2:6, which will be explained shortly, taps into the very nature of God's very Self. Who Jesus Christ was and is and what Jesus did on earth for us all express the heart of God.

Jesus is what God is like. In Jesus we see God most clearly. His life is the God-shaped life. To deny self-promotion in order to serve others is God-like and godly because it is Christ-like. Lynn Cohick calls us to begin this passage in a way that flows from the previous passage, beginning with the "If" statements in 2:1. That is, since we already are participating in Christ, let us live in a way that reflects the pattern of his life (Cohick, *Philippians*, 106). The common life into which we are called is nothing less than the God-life.

COMMON LIFE WITH ONE ANOTHER

In 2:1–4 Paul exhorted the Philippians to a unity rooted in humility that emerges from being in Christ. That observation rushed Paul immediately to how Jesus himself conducted himself, which he will set out in a series of poetic lines (notice how the NIV makes our passage poetic). The challenge is the foundational principle: in Christ we can have a common life that exhibits the way Jesus lived. Peter and John, it was said, impressed the authorities in Jerusalem as "ordinary men" who "had been with Jesus" (Acts 4:13). Others and outsiders who come into the circles of Christian fellowship will be most impressed if we look like we have spent time with Jesus.

COMMON LIFE IN THE HEART OF GOD

Paul now recites (and probably edits) in vv. 6–11 an early Christian poem, and perhaps a hymn, about the pattern of Jesus' life. And these lines were probably composed for early Christian worship and meditation. They sing into worship the teachings of Jesus himself (Mark 8:31–9:1; John 13; Hurtado, *At the Origins of Christian Worship*).* A Roman leader named Pliny observed not long after this letter was written that the Christians assembled to "sing hymns to Christ as if to a god" (Pliny, *Letters* 10.96.7). This poem in Philippians 2 could have been one of those hymns. It's worth remembering that, as Marilynne Robinson once said, "Caesar Augustus was also said to be divine" but "there aren't any songs about him" (Robinson, *When I was a Child I Read Books*, 127). We still sing about Jesus.

Here are the important words that take us to the common-life heart of God: "Who, being in the very nature God." The RSV, ESV, NRSV, NLT, and CEB have "though he was in the form of God" or something close. The word "though" expresses a concession. That is, *though* he was God and transcendent and invisible and immortal, nonetheless God condescended to become a human. This very

---

* Other passages in the New Testament claimed to be hymns or hymn fragments include John 1:1–18; Colossians 1:15–20; Ephesians 2:14–16; 1 Timothy 3:16; 2 Timothy 2:11–13; Titus 3:4–7; 1 Peter 3:18–22 plus the many songs of Revelation.

traditional interpretation impacted the history of how most Christians have read this text. The Greek behind this is not so explicit as "though" suggests.

Instead of "though," most recent translations have gone with what can be called a simple, literal translation: "being in the very nature God" (NIV 1984, TNIV, NIV 2011; see also KJV, ASV). "Being" is the plain sense of the term, no more and no less. The word behind "very nature" is *morphē*, which points to the defining, visible attributes of Jesus, including equality with God. Many today read "being" as pointing to something *innate and essential to who God is*. That is, it is God-like for God to extend himself out of love into human form in order to express that love (Gorman, *Inhabiting the Cruciform God*). It's complicated, but we need to get this right. Instead of "though," we should think like the meaning is this: *because* he was God, or *being the kind of God God was*, he became human to redeem humans.

Which reveals something profound about our God. God is and always has been and always will be a God who reaches out to others in self-giving love. God the Father loves God the Son and God the Spirit, and the Son loves the Father and the Spirit, and the Spirit loves the Son and the Father. In eternity past God has always been a self-giving God. This is why John says, "God *IS* love" (1 John 4:16 emphasis added). To love is to give oneself for another, and in loving to encircle them in a common life.

The implication of this reading boggles: we are to share a Christ-like common life *because God in God's own Self is a common-life self-giving God*. When we "have the same mindset as Christ Jesus" we experience the heart of God. In Philippians this had to do with such things as sharing resources with one another and supporting the gospel mission to reach others with that gospel. But the common life for them was so profound it affected every dimension of life.

COMMON LIFE EMBODIED IN CHRIST

God's very self-giving essence was embodied in the pattern of Jesus' own life. I was taught as a college student to read Philippians 2:6–11 as a "U": from the throne room of God's own inner life (2:6), down into human flesh (2:7), then down even further into the degradation of human degradations, death on a cross (2:8), which then turns upward into God's exaltation of Christ "to the highest place" (2:9) where the crucified One will be One worshiped by all and declared Lord of all (2:10–11). That's the U–from heaven to earth and back. (The downward-upward imagery, of course, is imagery and not reality. Heaven is no more upward than downward since heaven is wherever God is, and God is everywhere.)

This U-pattern reveals *Who God is* and how God acts. As Hawthorne and Martin express this poetically,

> "in the divine economy of things,
> by giving people receive,
> by serving they are served,
> by losing their lives they find them,
> by dying they live,
> by humbling themselves they are exalted"
>   (Hawthorne, *Philippians*, 133,
>   reformatted).

Jesus did not seize or hang on to "equality with God," and this text affirms as well as any other text in the Bible the deity of Christ (2:6). The NIV's "used to his own advantage" expresses the very heart of Paul's challenge to the Philippians. Instead of self-protection and self-promotion, Jesus chose other-protection and other-promotion. Instead of hanging on to glory, Jesus entered into the human condition all the way to the bottom. Nothing more ignominious can be experienced in the human condition than being a slave (not "servant" as in the NIV) and then, as a slave, suffering the vicious humiliation of the Roman powers crucifying naked and in public a just, good man, which was Jesus' fate among them.

Think about this: the Way of Jesus counters the Way of Rome, and the Way of Rome has had too much play among the Philippians. So Paul has to remind them all over again about the Way of Jesus. The Way of Jesus is the Way of God.

Notice that these were choices made by Jesus. He "did not consider equality" and "he made himself" and "by taking" and "he humbled himself." He consciously and intentionally chose the cross-shaped life (cruciformity) at each stage of the journey. The Son did not surrender divinity but became human *as the one equal to God*. He was the God-Human, not the Human formerly known as God. Just as mothers and fathers do not cease being parents when they lay on the floor to play with a child and so enter into that child's world. Jesus' choices are matched by the Father's choices to reward him: "God exalted him" and "gave him" so Jesus would be given the glory he deserved.

The challenge to unity through humility, to a Christoform life, is a choice. No, it is daily choices. In relationship with those we love and those we don't even like, at home, at play, at work, at church. In the ordinary and in the unusual. We experience glory on the far side of the cruciform life, though at times we glimpse that glory now.

QUESTIONS FOR REFLECTION AND APPLICATION

1. In what ways does Jesus show us what God is like?

2. How does God express God's love through a life-in-common?

3. What is the "U-shaped" pattern of Jesus' life?

4. In what ways does your life look like Jesus, like you have spent time with him?

5. What does "cruciform" mean? How can you live a more cruciform, or Christoform, life, especially regarding unity?

FOR FURTHER READING

Michael Gorman, *Inhabiting the Cruciform God* (Grand Rapids: Wm. B. Eerdmans, 2009).
Larry Hurtado, *At the Origins of Christian Worship* (Grand Rapids: Wm. B. Eerdmans, 2000).
Marilynne Robinson, *When I Was a Child I Read Books: Essays* (New York: Farrar, Straus and Giroux/Picador, 2013).

A COMMON LIFE
OF SACRIFICE

Philippians 2:12–18

¹² Therefore, my dear friends, as you have always obeyed—not only in my presence, but now much more in my absence—continue to work out your salvation with fear and trembling, ¹³ for it is God who works in you to will and to act in order to fulfill his good purpose.

¹⁴ Do everything without grumbling or arguing, ¹⁵ so that you may become blameless and pure, children of God without fault in a warped and crooked generation. Then you will shine among them like stars in the sky ¹⁶ as you hold firmly to the word of life. And then I will be able to boast on the day of Christ that I did not run or labor in vain. ¹⁷ But even if I am being poured out like a drink offering on the sacrifice and service coming from your faith, I am glad and rejoice with all of you. ¹⁸ So you too should be glad and rejoice with me.

Paul's big idea for the Philippians, intoxicated as some were with Rome's status-climbing way of life, was living a common life with one another shaped by the other-serving humility of Christ himself. That's a big idea, a bit abstract at times, and they may have wondered if it had legs. He's about to give them some legs so they walk straight toward the kingdom of God: they can respond to God's work, and they can cling to God's word.

RESPONDING TO GOD'S WORK

The core expression in 2:12–13 is "work out your salvation," with the NIV adding "continue to" because the verb has both a vivid sense as well as an intense engagement by each person in the assembly. "Work out" indicates human *responsibility* but that word "salvation" tends to trip up many readers. Cohick knows for many the wording here "registers a 9.0 on the theological Richter scale" (Cohick, *Philippians*, 133). Indeed, gluing the word "work" to "salvation" provokes a raised eyebrow or two for any Christian steeped in justification by faith (not works). Lower the eyebrow because what Paul means is this: Saved people live saved lives. In this context, a saved life is a Christoform-based unity with one another. That's what a saved life looks like because salvation is holistic: heart, mind, soul, body, personal and group.

Philippians 2:12–13 works just as 2:1–4 worked: since they are saved they are to live like the saved.

One can be tripped as well by the rather gloomy "with fear and trembling" (2:12). Bible readers may well recall this expression echoing what God's people experienced in God's presence (Exodus 15:16). But "fear and trembling" evokes not terror but an all-consuming reverence and awe and humility in the face of God's majesty and glory. Saved people put a saved life into effect in humility before a mighty God. Yet, let's not get too comfortable. God's sheer presence overwhelms us, prompting our sense of finitude and gratitude to be in God's presence.

Our responsibility before God is just that: *response-ability*. We respond to God's saving work in us because it is God's work in us to which we respond. Paul is not giving a 1st Century version of a "God helps those who help themselves." He's got a different mind, saying instead "for it is God"–not you, not me–"who works [or energizes] in you to will and to act" (2:13). God's energy in us promotes desire "to fulfill his good purpose." I prefer a translation of "good pleasure" or even "delight" over "purpose." Think of the Father's delight in the Son at the baptism of Jesus (Matthew 3:17). Think, then, not so much of God's working in us to accomplish something but of the Father working in us for God's delight in us and, by extension, our sheer pleasure of knowing and loving God. God works in us so we will find life's deepest joy and pleasure in God.

CLINGING TO GOD'S WORD

You can count on one hand the number of churches in the history of the church who have not had some "grumbling or arguing" (2:14) and the devastating impact of gossip and slander. Cohick says, "How tempting to tear another down . . . How subtly delicious to nibble on another's good reputation and eat away at it; we feel our own self nourished." She continues, "Yet in fact we are ingesting poison" (Cohick, *Philippians*, 151).

Like "fear and trembling," the term "grumbling" echoes the children of Israel in their march from Egypt to the promised land (Numbers 20:2–5). Notice what can happen though: if we avoid a grumbling posture toward unfulfilled (and sometimes mistaken) expectations we are taking steps toward "blameless and pure." Paul quotes

Deuteronomy 32:5 from that amazing Song of Moses, a song rehearsing God's steady faithfulness in the face of Israel's clunky faithfulness. But to those words of Moses, Paul inserts into Moses' negative words "without fault." Not only would they be without fault but they "will shine . . . like the stars" while they are surrounded in Philippi with a "warped and crooked generation" (Philippians 2:15). Paul has taken the words of Moses and made them fit his context because he wants them to "shine" with the light of the gospel, a shining that is both in word and deed. His words echo Jesus' own words (Matthew 5:14–16).

Great ideas, but surely we may be asking how we can do this.

We can discover a without-fault and shining-like-stars faithfulness if we "hold firmly" or *cling* to "the word of life" (2:16). We should not reduce the "word of life" to the Bible no matter how important the Bible is to us. Rather, this is Life itself's word, that is, the gospel about Jesus Christ. Jesus is both the Life himself and the one who gives life, and the life he gives works in us to form a life-fitting salvation. We can learn daily to cling to Jesus.

Paul has some personally invested goals. If they cling to Jesus as the word of Life itself, Paul will be able to stand proud "on the day of Christ," that is, the second coming (2:16). He suddenly flips a switch to anticipate that he may not live that long by saying "even if I am being poured out like a drink offering on the sacrifice" (2:17). The imagery is that drink offerings were poured out on the sacrifice at the altar, and here the Philippians are the sacrifice and Paul is the drink offering, which suggests Paul realizes he just may become a martyr for the faith (Bockmuehl, *Philippians*, 161). No matter for Paul: "I am glad and rejoice with all of you."

We can tie Paul's mixing of imagery together now. Christlikeness and salvation and sacrificial service are each one image of how the Philippians are to live a common life marked by humble other-centeredness, the very paradigm of God's own life embodied in Jesus Christ.

QUESTIONS FOR REFLECTION AND APPLICATION

1. How does the phrase "saved people live saved lives" help nuance the idea of "work out your salvation"?

2. What is Paul's view of sacrifice? How does he himself expect to be a sacrifice?

3. How does Paul alter Moses's words to fit Paul's context?

4. What does a "saved life" look like for you?

5. If God works in us to accomplish God's delight in us, how does that impact your view of your interactions with God? In what ways do you find pleasure and delight in God, and how do you experience God's delight in you?

A COMMON LIFE
OF CO-WORKERS

Philippians 2:19–3:1a

¹⁹ *I hope in the Lord Jesus to send Timothy to you soon, that I also may be cheered when I receive news about you.* ²⁰ *I have no one else like him, who will show genuine concern for your welfare.* ²¹ *For everyone looks out for their own interests, not those of Jesus Christ.* ²² *But you know that Timothy has proved himself, because as a son with his father he has served with me in the work of the gospel.* ²³ *I hope, therefore, to send him as soon as I see how things go with me.* ²⁴ *And I am confident in the Lord that I myself will come soon.*

²⁵ *But I think it is necessary to send back to you Epaphroditus, my brother, co-worker and fellow soldier, who is also your messenger, whom you sent to take care of my needs.* ²⁶ *For he longs for all of you and is distressed because you heard he was ill.* ²⁷ *Indeed he was ill, and almost died. But God had mercy on him, and not on him only but also on me, to spare me sorrow upon sorrow.* ²⁸ *Therefore I am all the more eager to send him, so that when you see him again you may be glad and I may have less anxiety.* ²⁹ *So then, welcome him in the Lord with great joy, and honor people like him,* ³⁰ *because he almost died for the*

work of Christ. He risked his life to make up for the help you
yourselves could not give me.
3:1 Further, my brothers and sisters, rejoice in the Lord!

An outsider in Philippi, after observing Paul and those in his inner circle, would describe that circle as "friends." Friendship was deeply valued in Philippi. Furthermore, it was discussed endlessly among the elite male circles. Friendship has been discussed for centuries (Enright and Rawlinson, *The Oxford Book of Friendship*). The two best thinkers in the ancient world about friendship were the Athenian philosopher Aristotle and the Roman orator Cicero. I quote only Cicero:

> For friendship is nothing else than an accord [or unity] in all things, human and divine, conjoined with mutual goodwill and affection, and I am inclined to think that, with the exception of wisdom, no better thing has been given to man by the immortal gods (Cicero, *De Amicitia* 6.20).

Friendship is about unity and emotional affection and is prized above all of life's blessings. Notice that "no better thing has been given" to humans than friendship. That's how high the Romans valued friendship. The word "friend" in friendship translates *philos*, which was one of the most popular terms for love in that world. C.S. Lewis famously talked about four loves, one of which was friendship. Friends voluntarily love one another and through that love for one another grow in virtue. It's a pity the writing about friendship has fallen off in the last half century.

But Paul *never once* called those in his inner circle

"friends." Sometime sit down for an afternoon and read especially the end of Paul's letters and compose a list of his "friends." There are dozens of names, but he never calls them "friends," while all those watching him thought they were his friends. Paul's top-of-the-list favorite term for Christians of all sorts was siblings or "brothers and sisters" (NIV), and his favorite term for his inner circle was "co-workers" (*sunergoi*). In this passage a window is opened on Paul's relationship with two of them, Timothy and Epaphroditus.* When I travel with students in Turkey and Greece, and one time to Rome and Pompeii, I give short talks on various co-workers of Paul (see McKnight, *Pastor Paul*, 31–78). The list includes Priscilla and Aquila, Urbanus, Timothy, Phoebe, Titus, Epaphroditus, Epaphras, Clement, Jesus called Justus, Philemon, Mark, Aristarchus, Demas, and Luke. We find in vignettes of his co-workers the relational heart of Paul, three of which chambers in that heart can be seen here.

CO-WORKERS AFFIRM ONE ANOTHER

Men, given as too many are to competition with one another, struggle to affirm other men. I'm not saying that's not true about women, but I do know a few fellow professors who seem never to be able to affirm the scholarly work of others. It's like if they do, they will lose some kind of status. The only ones such persons tend to affirm are those who praise their own work! Ugh. Paul knew a culture like that among the Romans. As one who cared about

---

* The name is connected to the goddess Aphrodite, which certainly indicates the man was a gentile convert to the gospel.

God's glory and who recognized God's gifts among us, the apostle practiced public commendation and affirmation of others. One can read Romans 16 to see numerous examples.

We who are men need to learn from Paul. Starting today.

Paul had no trouble affirming his co-workers in public. Here's what he says about Timothy in our passage: "I have no one else like him" and he has "genuine concern" for others, and he has "proved himself" as a "son" (2:20–22). In saying there is "no one like him," Paul uses a wonderful term: *isopsychos*, an equivalent person, a total equal, equal in soul. Now add verses like 1 Corinthians 4:17: "Timothy, my son [or child] whom I love, who is faithful in the Lord" and recall Paul thinks the younger man can be trusted to pass on Paul's teachings. He was often Paul's substitute (1 Thessalonians 3:2, 6). Again, 1:1 of Philippians shows just how close the two were: though the letter is in Paul's voice he makes Timothy a co-sender and co-author of the letter. That's how close they were: Paul's words and Timothy's words were so intermingled one could not discern who said what.

About Epaphroditus Paul says this: "my brother, co-worker and fellow soldier" whom the Philippians sent on to Paul (either to Rome or to Ephesus) to care for Paul. He's also one who "longs for all of you" so much that he is "distressed because you heard he was ill" and almost died. Paul loved the man so much that he says about Ephroditus's surviving a death scare, he was spared "sorrow upon sorrow." Epaphroditus' arrival in Philippi will relieve them of "anxiety" and they are to "honor people like him" because he "risked his life" so he could aid Paul when they could not (2:25–30). Epaphroditus delivered to Paul a financial gift from the Philippians (4:18), and now returning home probably carried this letter and then pastorally and persuasively read it to the Philippians. Many wonder why such a strong commendation is given for this man. We do not know for sure but it's just possible he was a "messenger" in the sense of an "apostle" who was sent to join Paul in the mission and through sickness or perhaps even lack of gifting was unable to sustain that mission (Osiek, *Philippians*, 78–79; Cohick, *Philippians*, 156–157).

Settle into your chair, and imagine you are in the church in Philippi. Now hear Paul speak of you like this when the letter is read. Does your chest not swell a bit? Do you not feel a sense of affirmation and a little rise in your self-esteem? Of course you do.

We need to do this more in our own circles, whether in churches or in our homes or in our workplaces. Public affirmations, so say the business leaders, make for a healthier work culture. The same is true for homes and churches. Not only can we learn to affirm one another, but we can learn to care for one another and to pitch in for one another.

Co-Workers Care for One Another

Paul says Timothy will "show genuine concern for your welfare" (2:20) in a world where "everyone looks out for their own interests, not those of Jesus Christ" (2:21). But not Timothy. He was other-oriented. Timothy also "served with" Paul "in the work of the gospel" (2:22). The word is stronger: he was "enslaved with" Paul in that work. Slavery was the color of water in those days so it was easy for them to describe their own relationship to one another and to Christ as slaves.

Epaphroditus was a "messenger" for the Philippians, a go-between, who arrived to care for Paul's needs, which probably indicates food and drink and clothing and news and conversation. Prisons didn't provide such things. When Epaphroditus heard the Philippians were sorrowed over his illness, he was sorrowed over their sorrow–such was the man's empathy and care for others. Paul himself was spared his own empathic sorrow when his co-worker survived death. The Philippians will be filled with joy when Epaphroditus arrives, and they will publicly affirm him (2:29; 3:1). At the heart of this man's care for others is that he risked his life because he loved Paul so much.

You may notice someone in your circle who hears what others do not hear. That someone is looking for a special kind of mask during the Covid-19 pandemic and sends them some. That someone loves a certain kind of coffee and so provides an anonymous gift card to their favorite café. That someone shows interest in Lil Copan's novel, *Little Hours*, and so another someone drops one in the mail to that other someone. Christians care for one another like this. It's the quotidian or routine stuff of life where care shows up.

Co-Workers Pitch in for One Another

Many attributes color in the lines between co-workers, including learning the gentle art of pitching in when another needs aid. Paul says of Epaphroditus that he risked death "to make up for the help you yourselves could not give me" (2:30). The word Paul uses here could be translated "fill up" the way one supplies the extra funds to someone when they are running short. Sunday School teachers do this; home Bible study leaders do this; parents do this for other parents; teachers do this for other teachers; neighbors do this; friends do this; and co-workers do this too.

When our friend Beth Allison Barr's church, located among those without great resources or means, was discovered to be running low during the pandemic . . . well, here's what happened. She passingly mentioned this on Twitter in the context of a not-so-pleasant situation and her "friends" all over the country–and let's call them co-workers, how about it?–erupted into nothing less than an avalanche of generosity for the church. Beth messaged me after giving a lecture at a university with a "Praise God!" and the astounding dollar amount.

Just like Epaphroditus, except for the risking one's life part!

Friends may pitch in like this, but co-workers do so even more. They form what Hawthorne and Martin call a "network of mutual service" (Hawthorne, *Philippians*, 158). Why? Because Christians and co-workers share a common life shaped by the Way of Christ (2:6–11). Our passage opened on this very tone: because Paul himself could not get to Philippi he planned soon to send Timothy to "fill up" what Paul had been doing and then to report back to Paul what was going on in Philippi (2:19). True enough but notice the opposite, too. Some were instead looking "out for their own interests" (2:21; look at 2 Timothy 4:10). He is probably pointing us back to the envy and rivalry problems of some gospel workers (Philippians 1:15–17). In other words, not like Christ who did not look to his own interests! Back to the good examples among Paul's co-workers. Before Timothy could be sent, Epaphroditus pitched in to take the long and hazardous trip to Philippi. Timothy and Paul would follow later (some think this may be recorded in Acts 20:1–6).

That's what friends are for. No, better. That's what Christians are for.

QUESTIONS FOR REFLECTION AND APPLICATION

1. How was friendship viewed in Paul's world?

2. What terms does Paul use for his friends instead of calling them "friends"? Why do you think he used those terms?

3. What does Paul say about his close colleagues Timothy and Ephaphroditus?

4. Who in your life has shown special care for you the way Epaphroditus cared for Paul? Or who have you cared for in those ways?

5. Have you had any special co-working relationships in your Christian life? What did you most value about those people and your interactions with each other?

FOR FURTHER READING

Lil Copan, *Little Hours: A Novel* (Falmouth, Mass.: One Bird Books, 2021).

D.J. Enright and David Rawlinson, eds., *The Oxford Book of Friendship* (New York: Oxford University Press, 1991).

C.S. Lewis, *The Four Loves* (New York: HarperOne, 2017).

A COMMON LIFE
OF CONFESSION

Philippians 3:1b-11

[1] It is no trouble for me to write the same things to you again, and it is a safeguard for you. [2] Watch out for those dogs, those evildoers, those mutilators of the flesh. [3] For it is we who are the circumcision, we who serve God by his Spirit, who boast in Christ Jesus, and who put no confidence in the flesh—[4] though I myself have reasons for such confidence.

If someone else thinks they have reasons to put confidence in the flesh, I have more: [5] circumcised on the eighth day, of the people of Israel, of the tribe of Benjamin, a Hebrew of Hebrews; in regard to the law, a Pharisee; [6] as for zeal, persecuting the church; as for righteousness based on the law, faultless.

[7] But whatever were gains to me I now consider loss for the sake of Christ. [8] What is more, I consider everything a loss because of the surpassing worth of knowing Christ Jesus my Lord, for whose sake I have lost all things. I consider them garbage, that I may gain Christ [9] and be found in him, not having a righteousness of my own that comes from the law, but that which is through faith in Christ—the righteousness that comes from God on the basis of faith. [10] I want to know Christ—yes, to know the power of his resurrection and participation in his sufferings,

becoming like him in his death, [11] and so, somehow, attaining to the resurrection from the dead.

No one has stronger criticisms of one's former life than a convert. Some talk about how bad of a sinner they were or how deep they were into drugs or money or alcohol or sexual escapades. Some talk about their former religion the way divorced people at times describe their ex. In my lifetime I've heard nothing less than vituperations and accusations for one's former Roman Catholic or Methodist or Presbyterian or just plain "liberal" church: "I was raised in that church and never once heard the gospel." As one who has done research in conversion stories, I've heard that tale more times than I can count. Nasty rhetoric about one's former life seems irresistible.

And always has been. Paul himself is such a person. He describes his past in a way that permits him to criticize his present opponents. That is, his past is where his opponents are now.

A STRONG ACCUSATION

The language ancients used for their opponents does not play well today. In fact, that kind of strong language, often calling one's enemy some animal, was only part of the prophetic toolbox. John the Baptist was harsh, Jesus was harsh, Peter was harsh, Revelation ramps up harshness, and Paul was harsh too. (If you really want to read harsh accusations against one's opponents, read what Luther and Calvin say about the Catholics and Anabaptists. Yikes.) I'm not excusing anyone, and I don't think we should talk like this about one another, but I do want us to see the harsh accusations of Paul in their context. What was said in their world may not be license to say the same in our world.

Paul opens chapter three with a line that quickly erupts with explosive clarity. He starts with, "It is no trouble for me" (3:1), which could be translated, "I have no hesitation" to write to you about these things. This rather sedate statement suddenly shifts in tone to, "Watch out for those dogs!" Then he adds "those evildoers, those mutilators of the flesh" (3:2). To call someone "dog," which is still an insult in Germany (along with *Schwein*, or swine), is an insult. That insult is unfolded into two categories, one moral ("evildoers") and the other about law observance ("mutilators of the flesh" refers to circumcising gentiles). Which makes it clear that some opponents of Paul in Philippi were law-observant Jewish Christians.

Here's another problem. Christians have easily slid from Jesus' exaggerated rhetoric about Pharisees to thinking all Jews are Pharisees. Then they mix into the bowl of group denunciations Paul's exaggerated rhetoric about "dogs." Then they drop the exaggerated talk of opponents to think all ordinary Jews are worthy of such condemnations and before long we have outright prejudice and racial hatred, the kind that saw Jews as Christ-killers. Then we have the Holocaust. This is the danger of exaggerated rhetoric, and it must be made clear right here. Be careful. Our world is not their world. These words don't work in our world.

What also must be emphasized, and this kicks the stool out from under many, is that Paul is not here opposing Jews *per se* nor is his beef with Judaism. Paul's heated rhetoric aims at *Christians who think gentiles or all believers must observe the law*. Those Christians were probably Jewish Christians, but it's not the Jewish part that concerns him.

One does not find here, then, an argument with another religion. Rather, Paul perceives a dangerous departure from the true gospel about Jesus Christ by Christians bent on being as zealous as Paul was in his former life about observing the law of Moses.

A STRONG CLAIM

Paul makes strong claims about his past so he can crush the claims of his opponents. He crushes them so he can magnify the gospel about Jesus Christ. Those are the two moves he makes in this passage.

Paul turns his past completely upside down when he says "we," not they, are the "circumcision." That is, the true circumcision is not fleshly removal of skin but serving "God by his Spirit" and those who "boast in Christ Jesus" and those "who put no confidence in the flesh" (3:3). These are all jabs at his Jewish Christian opponents who believe Paul has denied the law and cut into the core identity of Israel/Jews. (One reading of Galatians 3:19–29 reveals how Paul thinks about the topic.) Their "confidence in the flesh" is an appeal to their circumcision and, at the same time, a very strong criticism by Paul. For him, "flesh" is corrupted human flesh that rejects the Spirit and Jesus as their own Messiah.

But Paul decides to play their game of flesh confidence. He's a Jew of the Jews, Israelite of the Israelites, Hebrew of the Hebrews. When it comes to his style of Judaism, that is, which approach to law observance he embodies, he's a Pharisee. This meant someone who interpreted the law carefully by expanding it to spell things out more clearly, and thus someone who followed it scrupulously and strictly. Like Catholics, evangelicals, Presbyterians,

Methodists, and Baptists adhering to their very special group-taught traditions today. (Of course they each think they're right. That's the point.)

So committed had Paul been to law observance that he persecuted the church. He tops these strong claims off with the strongest of all claims. He puts forward the standard of standards, "righteousness." A righteous person–like Joseph (Matthew 1:19)–is one who consistently follows the law.* By Pharisee standards, Paul says he was "faultless," and Bockmuehl says it well: many "cringe at this claim" by Paul (Bockmuehl, *Philippians*, 202). Jews believed they could follow God's law; they believed failures were atoned for on the Day of Atonement. Sacrifices meant they were clean with respect to law observance. Those who lived like this were "faultless." This does not mean sinless. Paul had been a faultless sinner! These strong claims are not exaggerations, and neither are they claims to perfection. Have you ever heard someone say they are a *devout* Catholic or an *observant* Jew? That's the kind of claim Paul was making about his past.

His various claims were also boundary markers between Jews and gentiles that became symbols of one's radical commitment to Israel's God and to God's law. They function then as public statements of one's allegiance. Much the way daily devotions, or weekly church attendance, or serving in a homeless shelter do in our world. Such practices identify us and mark us off from others who don't do such things.

So Paul's boundary-marking claims are strong: he was initiated into the covenant by law observant parents; he's from the innermost tribes (Judah, Benjamin); he can speak

---

* The NIV 1984 had "righteous" for Joseph but in the NIV 2011 it is "faithful to the law."

and read Hebrew; he's a Pharisee; his zeal has no limits; and when it gets right down to it, he was a totally observant Pharisee. There is no duplicity here. Paul was not a man crushed by a guilty conscience. Paul was not worried about going to heaven when he died. He was not in fear of losing his salvation. That man had a robust confidence in his God, in the law, and in his faithfulness to it. No, he didn't convert to Christ to assuage guilt. He converted because he met Jesus. That encounter shattered his old way of life.

Think about it this way: he magnified his Jewishness; he boasted about his faithfulness. Not as personal bragging but so he can speak to his law-observant opponents, best them, and then say, "In spite of all my zeal, I was wrong. I did not know that the church's gospel was right. Jesus met me, and I now know that he is the Messiah. That means my former zeal was misguided." Which then implies, "So is yours. So is theirs."

A STRONG CONFESSION

His former way of life was shattered by an entirely new perspective: what were "gains" are now a "loss" (3:7–8). The term will reverberate among some of his opponents all the way back to Jerusalem. A term that will be heard in synagogues all over the Mediterranean is that Paul considers his former law-observant life as "garbage." The Greek term is *skubala*. Some wonder here if this might be a momentary cuss word for Paul, something like "crap" or its more vulgar alternative that rhymes with "skit." The term, however, is best translated as *feces. Skubala* was used in medical manuals for excrement tossed into the garbage. So his former life was trashed.

What matters now is "knowing Christ Jesus my Lord"

(3:8). The *person-centeredness* of this expression cannot be missed. His faith is in a real person, the man from Galilee who walked its hills and taught in parables and opened doors to the table fellowship inside some had never imagined possible. Who made astounding claims for himself and worked wonders and miracles and healed people outside and inside homes. Who entered Jerusalem in protest, was crucified, was buried, and was raised and then ascended to the right hand of the Father. The gospel is about Jesus the person, not just what he accomplished. The gospel is not a set of ideas but a living, breathing incarnation of God. He is the One Paul now knows, and knowing Jesus has transformed his life.

On this side of his conversion, he is "in him," and that means his righteousness is not Pharisee-based law observance but the righteousness that comes "through faith in Christ . . . that comes from God on the basis of faith" (3:9). We hear a new echo of "not by works of the law but by faith," a very common expression on Paul's lips in the days of writing Galatians and Romans. He wants to "know Christ" in his fullness. Paul wants to know "the power of his resurrection" and that means he wants to know–think about this slowly–"participation in his sufferings" so he can, like Jesus, be "like him in his death." Because the death of Jesus–remember the U-shaped theology of 2:6–11–led to his exaltation, so Paul knows if he participates in his death he will also participate in his resurrection and be raised from among the dead.

Paul's writing leaps and bounds and shifts and turns and returns. So readers have to grip his letters tightly and hang on for all those moves. We started with his calling his opponents "dogs," and we find him on the near side of his former life where he is so in tune with Jesus he wants the pattern of Jesus' life to shape his own life. He's ready to die because the One who has died is the One who was raised. His confidence in the flesh never attained the kind of confidence he now finds in Jesus.

QUESTIONS FOR REFLECTION AND APPLICATION

1. How does Paul use his strong rhetoric about his former life to denounce his opponents? What is his linguistic and confessional strategy here?

2. Who is Paul criticizing and opposing in this passage?

3. How has Christian rhetoric been used to move beyond Paul's intent here into demonizing Jews?

4. What "group-taught traditions" or "boundary mark-ers" do you notice in your own denomination of Christianity?

5. What is your conversion tale? How did you come to follow Jesus? How have you told your story in the past, and how has this lesson impacted how you might tell that story in the future?

A COMMON LIFE
OF IMITATION

Philippians 3:12–4:1

[12] Not that I have already obtained all this, or have already arrived at my goal, but I press on to take hold of that for which Christ Jesus took hold of me. [13] Brothers and sisters, I do not consider myself yet to have taken hold of it. But one thing I do: Forgetting what is behind and straining toward what is ahead, [14] I press on toward the goal to win the prize for which God has called me heavenward in Christ Jesus.

[15] All of us, then, who are mature should take such a view of things. And if on some point you think differently, that too God will make clear to you. [16] Only let us live up to what we have already attained.

[17] Join together in following my example, brothers and sisters, and just as you have us as a model, keep your eyes on those who live as we do. [18] For, as I have often told you before and now tell you again even with tears, many live as enemies of the cross of Christ. [19] Their destiny is destruction, their god is their stomach, and their glory is in their shame. Their mind is set on earthly things. [20] But our citizenship is in heaven. And we eagerly await a Savior from there, the Lord Jesus Christ, [21] who, by the power that enables him to bring everything under

his control, will transform our lowly bodies so that they will be like his glorious body.

4:1 Therefore, my brothers and sisters, you whom I love and long for, my joy and crown, stand firm in the Lord in this way, dear friends!

Educators know that students learn more by watching and doing than by reading or listening. You can't always tell the teachers know this by the way they (or I) teach. Not to dismiss either listening or reading, but think about this: you can't learn to hit a golf ball long and straight by reading a Ben Hogan book, nor can you learn to make risotto by watching Natasha's Kitchen. You have to make some risotto and fail; and taste to see what *al dente* feels like. You don't learn to teach by reading about teaching but by teaching and embracing feedback from both students and seasoned teachers. The ancient world had a term for this: *imitation.* You learn best by seeing and then trying to do it.

Paul has enough chutzpah to use himself as an example to be imitated. His most famous statement like this is 1 Corinthians 11:1, "Follow my example," and he justifies that bold claim by deflecting himself to "as I follow the example of Christ." In our passage Paul completes his previous personal conversion story, which we looked at in the previous study, by admitting "not that I have already obtained all this" (Philippians 3:12). He says this three times if you want to count them in vv. 12–13.

In this passage he becomes the classic model of teaching by imitation. He tells us *what he does* (3:12–14) before he turns to *what we can all do by imitating him* (3:15–4:1). That's what I mean by chutzpah.

WHAT HE DOES

In denying his full-on arrival at perfect kingdom living three times, he states twice what he is doing before the kingdom's arrival. What he does is "press on" (3:12 and 3:14). "Press on" is not as colorful as the Greek term itself, which could be translated "I chase" or "I pursue." Behind the word "press on" (Greek *diōkō*) stands the very same term Paul just used in 3:6 for the intensity of his zeal, there translated as "persecuting." What he wants the Philippians to imitate is his passion, his zeal, his pursuit, his running after. He pursues "that for which Christ Jesus took hold of me" (3:12), which he explains in verse 14: "the goal to win the prize for which God has called me heavenward in Christ Jesus." He uses the image of the laurel wreath, which is the prize in running races. But it's an image of a transformed body fit for the kingdom itself. Jesus "will transform our lowly bodies so that they will be like his glorious body" (3:21). (Paul discusses this transformation extensively in 1 Corinthians 15:35–57 and 2 Corinthians 5:1–5, which you might read to fill in the picture of Philippians.) He does not believe in a spirit-only or soul-only eternal existence. We will not be ghost-like. He believes in the body but a body-that-is-transformed for a new existence. Call it Body 7.0, with seven as the Bible's perfect number.

He attaches two ideas to his pursuit: he forgets "what is behind," and he strains for "what is ahead" (3:13). The behind-him life points us back to his former high-status accomplishments in a life of radical law observance (3:4–6); the "what is ahead" is that glorious body future (3:21).

His pursuit then can be summarized like this: He is pursuing being with Christ; he is no longer pursuing status as an observant Pharisee; he is pursuing a life that is worthy of being with Christ forever; he is pursuing a life that defies death because it affirms the resurrection; and he is pursuing a body that swallows up what our bodies are now to become kingdom-shaped bodies fit for an embodied kingdom life.

In his desire to help them imitate a good Christian example, Paul shifts from what he does to what we can all do.

WHAT WE CAN ALL DO

"All of us, then, who are mature should take such a view of things" (3:15). The term "mature" almost suggests one who has reached one's goal, but such an accomplishment creates serious tension with the same term in 3:12 where Paul says he has most clearly *not* "arrived at my goal." This English translation "mature" helpfully corrects the KJV's "perfect," a translation that, as Lyn Osiek writes, "inspired generations of frustration" (Osiek, *Philippians*, 96). Maybe instead of either full perfection or even complete maturity Paul means "those of us committed to the goal of final perfection." At any rate, the "mature" are those in the pursuit of the king and his kingdom.

He now gets right to the heart of imitation, instructing them to "join together in following *my* example" (3:17). This can be translated more concisely as "become co-imitators of me!" since (he adds) "as you have *us* as a model," and that means at least Paul and Timothy and probably others in his circle. Notice what he does here. It's important to see that Paul is not self-absorbed. He widens the circle to imitate with "keep your eyes on those who live as we do" (3:17). He has broadened worthy examples to all who are in the pursuit of the kingdom. Not just imitating himself, but Christ and all those following Christ. Lynn Cohick helpfully gives us an image to think about here: Paul's model for education is not the teacher-student image but the master-apprentice relationship (Cohick, *Philippians*, 194–197). Another help for me comes from Osiek, who gets this just right when she says, "Paul never poses himself as an end but rather as a means to Christ" (Osiek, *Philippians*, 101).

Imitation as genuine education is a splendid idea if your example is Paul, the embattled apostle. You may already know the drill about Paul: he arrives in a new city, goes to the synagogue, preaches the gospel, some turn to Jesus as Messiah, some gentiles believe, Paul does not require observance of the law for the gentiles, some are not happy about Paul's liberal stance–opposition ensues. Everywhere he went he experienced people who didn't like him and who gossiped about him and who did what they could to discredit him. (Read 2 Corinthians 10–13 someday. Nearly every verse echoes the harsh words of his critics.) "Many live as enemies of the cross of Christ" (3:18). We have to guess who these "enemies" are but probably the ones mentioned in 1:15–18 and the dogs of 3:2. He now fills in the picture of his opponents with a few choice put-downs: they're headed toward final "destruction" and "their god is their stomach" and "their glory is their shame" (3:19). That is, their pursuit is "earthly things."

Their earthly pursuit contrasts with Paul's heavenly pursuit, even if the heavenly one occurs in the heat of opposition. Imitating Paul, friends, was chancy, and I'm not sure we think about this often enough. He faces opposition and death; his opponents cave to the opposition and join it. He faces it because his political kingdom citizenship is "in heaven," and on earth the believers are forming into kingdom colonies (3:20; see Gupta, "Living as Good Citizens," 302). A heaven-shaped pursuit requires what Michael Gorman calls a "bifocal" life: one that looks all the time in two directions–at both the first, earthly life of Jesus and at the second coming of Christ (Gorman, *Becoming the Gospel*, 65-79).

Let's tie this now together. Paul's goal (3:12), what he takes hold of (3:12), the heavenward prize (3:14), the heavenly citizenship (3:20), and what he waits for (3:20) has the "power that enables him to bring everything" into its proper order with Jesus as the Lord (3:21). That's the example he's urging others to follow. To imitate Paul then is to "seek first his kingdom" (Matthew 6:33), to pursue a life now that approximates the heavenly kingdom then. It is to live like Christ.

One more consideration before we close shop on this passage. Try reading Philippians 2:6–11 and then read the last few verses of chapter three. If one asks what it means to live like the Jesus of 2:6–11 our passage is a plain speech example of what that means.

QUESTIONS FOR REFLECTION AND APPLICATION

1. As Paul offers himself as an example to be followed, what kinds of things does he say about himself and what he does?

2. What does Paul mean when he invites the Philippians to imitate him and others, like Timothy, who "live as we do"?

3. How does imitation work as a form of education?

4. Who has served for you as a model to imitate in the Christian life as you seek to become more like Jesus? What have you learned from them?

5. How are you serving as a model for others? Who are you discipling, and how are you leading them to become more like Jesus as they imitate your example?

FOR FURTHER READING

Michael Gorman, *Becoming the Gospel* (Grand Rapids: Eerdmans, 2015), 302.

Nijay Gupta, "Living as Good Citizens of the Gospel Kingdom of Christ according to Philippians," in Nijay Gupta, Tara Beth Leach, Matthew W. Bates, and Drew J. Strait, *Living the King Jesus Gospel: Discipleship and Ministry Then and Now* (Eugene, Oregon: Cascade, 2021), 65–79.

A COMMON LIFE
OF UNITY, JOY,
AND PEACE

Philippians 4:2–9, 21–23

² I plead with Euodia and I plead with Syntyche to be of the same mind in the Lord. ³ Yes, and I ask you, my true companion, help these women since they have contended at my side in the cause of the gospel, along with Clement and the rest of my co-workers, whose names are in the book of life.

⁴ Rejoice in the Lord always. I will say it again: Rejoice! ⁵ Let your gentleness be evident to all. The Lord is near. ⁶ Do not be anxious about anything, but in every situation, by prayer and petition, with thanksgiving, present your requests to God. ⁷ And the peace of God, which transcends all understanding, will guard your hearts and your minds in Christ Jesus.

⁸ Finally, brothers and sisters, whatever is true, whatever is noble, whatever is right, whatever is pure, whatever is lovely, whatever is admirable—if anything is excellent or praiseworthy—think about such things. ⁹ Whatever you have learned or received or heard from me, or seen in me—put it into practice. And the God of peace will be with you.

²¹ Greet all God's people in Christ Jesus. The brothers and sisters who are with me send greetings. ²² All God's people here send you greetings, especially those who belong to Caesar's household.

23 The grace of the Lord Jesus Christ be with your spirit. Amen.

Special Note to the Reader: The text and commentary for Philippians 4:10–20 are found at the beginning of the Bible study on pp. 7–8.

Paul often begins to end his letters a page or two before he finally signs off. He's at times more like the preacher who seems to have two or three or four endings before ending. His "Finally" in verse eight then is but the beginning of "Finally." In this beautiful first-of-his-final sections three of his favorite themes in this letter come to expression again: unity (4:2–3), joy (4:4–7) and peace (4:8–9).

UNITY

It's good to start with the last line of this first paragraph, that is, with the end of verse three. He will soon mention three names and a number of others who are unnamed, and he reminds them that all their names are "in the book of life" (4:3). We can nurture unity with those with whom we disagree when we begin with a profound reality: we will live with one another in peace in the final kingdom of God.

The first two names surprise us. We have not heard of these women before but mentioning their names may well make us wonder if their contentions with one another were at work in other passages. Many think so. The name Euodia means "Ms. Good Path" and Syntyche means "Ms. Fortune." Cool names aside, Paul knows they are at odds with one another. He wants them to "be of the same mind"

(4:2), which means to come to some kind of agreement. We can't be sure what they were on about, though many suggestions have been made, including how to relate their own social status to living as a Christian in Philippi or perhaps they were battling in court.

Asking two people at odds to agree often does not do it as it involves compromise, and often each believes her position is principled and right. Knowing this, Paul asks a specific unnamed person ("you"), whom he calls his "true companion" or the one with whom he is "harnessed together," to nurture reconciliation. But then we get some more information about the situation. Euodia and Syntyche have competed with Paul in gospel mission work along with "Clement" and other "co-workers," his favorite term for his inner circle of gospel missioners. This puts these two women inside the circle of co-workers, which means gospel workers—evangelizing, teaching, planting churches, praying, visiting, offering hospitality, raising funds, and more beside. Were they deacons? Were they household leaders of different house churches? (Cohick, *Philippians*, 209–210) Were they bishops? (Osiek, *Philippians*, 111–112) What is clear, as Osiek observed, is that they are not just bickering women, which is a sexist observation by too many (Osiek, *Philippians*, 112), but leaders of significance in Philippi. Their tension taxed the assemblies.

JOY

Paul's own imprisonment turned him into an agent of joy. Just look at the following verses in this short letter to see how often he brings up joy: 1:4, 18, 25; 2:2, 17–18, 28, 29; 3:1; 4:1, 4, 10. Again, someone say "persecution," and Paul answers back with "joy." This is not a mental trick, even if the happiness project works for some. No, this is a joy "in the Lord" because, as he tells them in the next verse, the Lord's coming is "near." Joy transcends our sense of happiness when happiness slides into smiley faces or giddiness. Joy is a disposition and an emotion of seeing the present in light of the final kingdom of God and the lordship of Jesus right now. The End's "all will be well" opens the door to joy.

Joy in whatever we face leads Paul to encourage those in Philippi to a list of healthy practices in the midst of social tension over the gospel and the church. The temptation is to get busy doing something about it—contacting the authorities, public debates in the marketplace, and worry worry worry. No Paul says, resume your life, avoid aggressiveness, and form a "gentleness . . . evident" to the public (4:5). How? Turn to communion with God as the antidote to inner turbulence, which is my translation for "anxious." What might that be? What wakes you up in the middle of the night that will not let you fall back into sleep? What raises your blood pressure and makes your face go flush? What makes you tense and makes your palms sweat and what turns at times into anxiety attacks? The first century philosopher Seneca once said, "The fact that the body is lying down is no reason for supposing that the mind is at peace" (Seneca, *On Noise*, 6). He had to know. The man was in the inner circle of the emperor.

Now I have wandered into something that in many cases will need more than someone telling you to pray more. I don't believe that Paul provides a full "cure for worry" (Hawthorne, *Philippians*, 255). "Do not be anxious" is not about anxiety disorders or trauma-related panic attacks. At times we will need a therapist to help us identify our anxieties and their roots, a therapist who can guide us into better coping skills–like rest, relaxation, exercise, better eating habits, cognitive-behavioral or trauma therapies, and perhaps medication.

And prayer. In Marilynne Robinson's wonderful novel, *Lila*, the narrator says of the lead character who observes her pastor husband praying. "She meant to ask him sometime how praying is different from worrying. His face was about as strained and weary as it could be, white as it could be" (Robinson, *Lila*, 234). Few tie prayer and worry together so tightly, but that's to the detriment of the many. They go together.

Paul does not know what we know about therapy, but he does know prayer has helped him immensely. It has helped many of us. Regardless, "in every situation," he says, we can turn to God in "prayer and petition" and just plain ask God for help (4:6). Prayers of petitions in the history of the church have formed into what is called a "collect," a formal prayer of request (McKnight, *To You All Hearts Are Open*). It begins by naming God (Father, God Almighty, etc.), it then says something to God about God that reminds God of a truth about God that forms a solid foundation for the request. So we have "Father, you are the transcendent and utterly calm God of all creation and you know all things. . . ." Then it turns to the request: "Calm my heart and mind and relieve my anxieties." This is then followed by a commitment for the one praying: "That I may do what you have called me to do more effectively, less anxiously, and more victoriously." And Christian prayers always finish with something like "through Christ our Lord, Amen."

Nothing has been more calming and soothing in my own soul than the collects of the church and pondering God in the midst of my own anxious moments.

PEACE

Finishing his encouragement to pray (4:6–7), no surprise here, is the claim that prayer promotes peace (4:7), which leads Paul to another "Finally" about doing the right things. In doing the right things "the God of peace will be with you" (4:9). So, peace begins and ends this exhortation to do the right things. What are the right things, which are right-er when done as well at the right time?

> Whatever is true,
> Whatever is noble,
> Whatever right,
> Whatever is pure,
> Whatever is lovely,
> Whatever is admirable.
> If anything is excellent or praiseworthy . . .

What a splendid list of eight virtues, any of which can remind us of what the right thing may be for us to do!

Paul urges the Philippians to think positive thoughts: "think about such things" and not about the sources and causes of our anxieties. I confess that what often has calmed my soul in the middle of the night is not these wonderful virtues but standing near a golf green and chipping balls onto the green. Which was an improvement for me over my mother's instruction to me as a child, which may have been yours: Count sheep. And think about it, sheep are covered with an abundance of wool, wool makes me itch and get warm, and that doesn't help me get to sleep at all. Golf does.

Paul returns to the theme of imitation (see above at 3:12–4:1) to close this passage with one more "whatever," and this one is "whatever you have learned or received or heard from him, or seen in me—put into practice" (4:9). This whatever reduces those eight virtues above to one: imitation of a wise person. The best way to grow is to imitate the one who has grown.

SIGNING OFF

As you may remember, we began this study guide by looking at 4:10–20 as the gateway into this wonderful letter. Skipping that passage now, we turn to the end. He wants them to greet "God's people in Christ Jesus." The siblings who are near Paul in his imprisonment send their greetings too (4:21). In fact, "all God's people" in Rome with Paul share their greetings, but Paul mentions a special group when he says, "especially those who belong to Caesar's household" (4:22). It appears Paul is in custody of the emperor and some of those who are guarding him are in the employ of the emperor Nero. Some of those have converted to the gospel about Jesus through Paul's witness. The Book of Acts told that very story of the gospel's expansion from Jerusalem all the way to Rome.

After all this letter's emphasis on generosity and gift giving, we cannot avoid hearing something about gift giving when Paul signs off with "the *grace* [that is, the gift of God's grace] of our Lord Jesus Christ," who is grace embodied, "be with your spirit. Amen" (4:23).

QUESTIONS FOR REFLECTION
AND APPLICATION

1. What have you been taught or assumed about Euodia and Syntyche in the past? How does this study impact your view of them?

2. What are the conflicts and worries in your life that threaten to choke out unity and joy?

3. How has prayer comforted you when you were anxious?

4. In addition to prayer, what other gifts of experience, rest, and science have brought peace to your worry?

5. What have you learned about the common life shared together with others in Christ through this study?

FOR FURTHER READING

Scot McKnight, *To You All Hearts Are Open* (Brewster, Mass.: Paraclete, 2021).

Marilynne Robinson, *Lila* (New York: Farrar, Straus and Giroux, 2014).

Seneca, "On Noise," in P. Lopate, *The Art of the Personal Essay* (New York: Anchor, 1995), 5–8.

1 & 2 THESSALONIANS

INTRODUCTION:
READING PAUL'S LETTERS
TO THE THESSALONIANS

Paul's first letter to the Thessalonians communicates to them after he established the church in Philippi, Paul's first "European" church. All of this is recorded in Acts 16–17. Most of us today know about Athens but few know that Thessaloniki is a massive city today. By the way, it is pronounced thes-SAHL-uh-nee-kee. It's on a major Roman road, as was Philippi, starting at the end of Rome's Via Appia to modern Turkey called the Via Egnatia. It was Rome's *Autobahn*. Thessalonica and its surrounding villages' population approximated 100,000, which gave Paul plenty of opportunity for his tentmaking skills. Working one's job is important in this letter. Crowded cities in the first century were also crowded with religions, including Judaism, and philosophies. Temples and idols were a constant.

I like this letter for its wonderful narrative of pastor Paul's relationship to the church. Only in 2 Corinthians do we read anything quite like it. That narrative can be gleaned from 1 Thessalonians 1:2–3:13, basically the first three chapters, which makes up almost half of this letter. So in reading, keep your eyes open for Paul as a pastor talking to one of his churches. He gets down to his major exhortation only at 4:1 (that they live to please God), and then answers two important questions about the return of Christ (4:13–5:11), and then signs off his letter from 5:12–28. Paul discusses the return of Christ more extensively because the Thessalonians got his teachings messed up.

Paul was either in Athens (notice 3:1, 6) or more probably in Corinth (Acts 18:5) when he wrote and sent this letter to Thessalonica, and it appears it was sent then in 50 AD or so.

Paul's second letter to the Thessalonians is both like and unlike the first letter. There are some pastoral touches in 2 Thessalonians like the emphasis on being "brothers and sisters" or family members, but there are not as many pastoral moments in the second as in the first letter, and the topic of eschatology–about the second coming–in the second letter augments 1 Thessalonians. Here we must anchor the ship: these letters have taught Christians since the 1st Century to live a life that is altogether shaped by confidence in what God will do but to live that life without trying to

escape from this world. Kingdom living is the shape of life now, which means a life that counters the life of the Roman world. These two letters are particularly concerned with how followers of Jesus conduct themselves sexually.

Commentaries cited in the Study Guide (throughout the Guide you will find the author's name and title as noted in this book listing with page numbers whenever I cite something from it):

Timothy A. Brookins, *First and Second Thessalonians* (Paideia Commentaries; Grand Rapids: Baker Academic, 2021). [Brookins, *1–2Thess*)]

John Byron, *1 and 2 Thessalonians* (Story of God Bible Commentary; Grand Rapids: Zondervan, 2014). [Byron, *1–2Thess*)]

Gordon Fee, *The First and Second Letters to the Thessalonians* (New International Commentary on the New Testament; Grand Rapids: Wm. B. Eerdmans, 2009). [Fee, *1–2Thess*)]

Beverly Roberts Gaventa, *First and Second Thessalonians* (Interpretation; Louisville: John Knox, 1998; cited from the Kindle edition). [Gaventa, *1–2Thess*)]

Nijay K. Gupta, *1 & 2 Thessalonians* (Critical Introductions to the New Testament; Grand Rapids: Zondervan, 2019). [Gupta, *1–2Thess*)]

Michael W. Holmes, *1 & 2 Thessalonians* (NIV Application Commentary: Grand Rapids: Zondervan, 1998). [Holmes, *1–2Thess*)]

AFFIRMING
OTHERS

1 Thessalonians 1:1–10

¹ Paul, Silas and Timothy,

To the church of the Thessalonians in God the Father and the Lord Jesus Christ: Grace and peace to you.

² We always thank God for all of you and continually mention you in our prayers. ³ We remember before our God and Father your work produced by faith, your labor prompted by love, and your endurance inspired by hope in our Lord Jesus Christ.

⁴ For we know, brothers and sisters loved by God, that he has chosen you, ⁵ because our gospel came to you not simply with words but also with power, with the Holy Spirit and deep conviction. You know how we lived among you for your sake. ⁶ You became imitators of us and of the Lord, for you welcomed the message in the midst of severe suffering with the joy given by the Holy Spirit. ⁷ And so you became a model to all the believers in Macedonia and Achaia. ⁸ The Lord's message rang out from you not only in Macedonia and Achaia—your faith in God has become known everywhere. Therefore we do not need to say anything about it, ⁹ for they themselves report what kind of reception you gave us. They tell how you turned to God from idols to serve the living and true God, [10] and to wait for his Son from heaven, whom he raised from the dead—Jesus, who rescues us from the coming wrath.

Many readers of Paul's letters skim his opening greetings, but these portions of his letters reward careful readers. The letter is written by three people, not just Paul. Paul, Silas, and Timothy are the writers. Paul gets the credit, but they are co-authors. In this book, I will often say "Paul" as most do, but we need also to remember his co-authors. The letter was carried by a courier who, in some cases, read the letter to the churches. Such a public reading was a performance, or what is sometimes called an "oral interpretation," with pauses and stops and looking over the audience and gestures and fluctuating of voice and tone. Those listening would have participated by verbal responses and questioning looks on the face and harumphing, at times interrupting to ask questions. (So very much *not* like our reading of the Bible on Sunday morning where we sit like little knobs on a frog's back.) The reader, called a *lector*, would have adlibbed when she or he considered it necessary to make sure everyone understood. You can be sure some of Paul's letters took a good long while to get through.

The church listening to this letter, the authors write, has a spiritual location: "in" both the "Father" and "the Lord Jesus Christ" (1:1). Their greeting is "grace and peace to you," two common words in the Greek world that had deep meanings for the early Christians.

"Why did he write us?" and "What does Paul have to say?" were the questions some in Thessalonica were asking when they gathered to hear this letter read. They will find out in what is nothing less than a pastoral narrative about Paul's relationship with them. The passage above is a wonderful *affirmation* of them.

AFFIRMING THEM IN PRAYER

Jews of Paul's day practiced a sacred rhythm of praying three times a day, and Paul's conversion to Jesus as Messiah did not interrupt his prayer rhythm a minute. Saying "always" and "continually" (or "incessantly") does not mean all day long, but in each of his times of prayer, he expressed thanksgiving to God for them. His prayers combined the customary prayers recited from memory, like the "Hear O Israel" (*Shema*), but also spontaneous prayers for anything that came to mind. Kris and I pray for family and friends and students and their families before our dinner. We both know the encouragement when folks tell us they pray for us, and we know that others say the same when we tell them we pray for them.

AFFIRMING THEIR VIRTUES

Though the NIV translates "We remember," the term "remember" is actually connected to "We always thank God." That is, he expresses thanksgiving for them to God *by* remembering them before God. His thanksgiving is a remembering. What he remembers about them before God is their three cardinal Christian virtues:

Faith ("your work of faith"),
Love ("your labor prompted by love"),
and Hope ("your endurance inspired by hope").

In saying he remembers their "work (NIV adds "produced by") of faith" we hear some of Paul's most important and contested terms. Many by now know that "works" when attached to "faith" breaks out into a Protestant rash, but Paul will have none of that nervousness about "work." For him "faith" is an act of turning to God in Christ and trusting God and becoming an allegiant follower of Jesus. This kind of "work of faith" does not merit redemption by human activity but expresses human agency in trusting Christ. Paul is thus reminding God of their conversions and their faithful discipleship. Faith is an "orientation of the whole self–of both thoughts and behaviors–toward the God of Jesus Christ" (Brookins, *1–2Thess*, 31).

To combine "love" with "labor" may well have elicited some chuckles among the parents and among those struggling to get along with one another. So true: to love another person in Christ is not an easy idealistic romance but a rugged commitment to spend time with another person, to be an advocate for that person as a person, and to grow together in their allegiance to Christ. Some days are easier than others; some days one wants to give up and go live on island or in a monastery. Human relations are both the joy of life and the grime pits of despair. Say it with two emphases: the *labor* of love, the labor of *love*.

He also affirms their "endurance of [NIV adds "inspired by"] hope" that is oriented on the return of "our Lord Jesus Christ" (1:3). Hope does not mean "I hope the Cleveland Guardians will win the World Series this year" nor does it mean hoping against all odds, and neither is hope the odds of a good chance. Rather, hope is a steadying virtue in life as one learns to look through the sufferings and troubles and relational challenges, that is, looking through all these to the final joys and glories of the kingdom of God, the New Jerusalem, where all will be well. John Byron speaks of hope as waiting (Byron, *1–2Thess*, 50–51). Death defeated, the Dragon doomed, and peace and justice and love and wisdom flourishing across the land forever and ever, "in which every chapter is better than the one before" (C.S. Lewis, *The Last Battle*). That's hope. It's confident and assured and still waiting.

Paul affirms the Thessalonians by publicly speaking well of their faith, love, and hope. He continues.

AFFIRMING THEIR EXEMPLARY LIFE

Paul affirms that God has chosen them because he, along with Silas and Timothy, watched the power of the gospel take hold in their personal lives and among them as a group. That gospel-taking-hold was "not simply with words," that is affirming truths of the gospel. No, the gospel took hold of them "with power, with the Holy Spirit, and with deep conviction" (1:5). Their conversions were the kind that stick, that dig deep roots, that change lives and conversations and marriages and relationships. A big word here is "Spirit," used in this context because the effectiveness of the gospel was so powerful the "only explanation I can find" is God's Spirit at work. Another big word here is "gospel," often translated "good news." The word refers to the preaching about Jesus, telling his story as the fulfillment of Israel's story (1 Corinthians 15:1–8). His story is about his life and teachings and death and burial and resurrection and ascension as the world's Savior and true Lord (McKnight, *King Jesus Gospel*).

The example of Paul, Silas, and Timothy (he says "we" not "my") in daily living became an embodiment of gospel living so much the Thessalonians "became imitators" both of them and the Lord. Emulation of good models is the deepest form of education, but for Paul imitation was not just of them but of those who were following Christ (1 Corinthians 11:1). A contemporary observed that "people put more trust in their eyes than in their ears," that is, what they observe in examples than what they hear from them (Seneca, *Letters* 6.5). What young Christians need most are good models of Jesus followers, people's lives that embody the way of Christ, and who are then worthy of being copied.

This imitation was in the midst of suffering and opposition to the gospel, which ramped up what it meant to get baptized, to participate in the house churches, to associate with other Jesus followers, and to turn away from "idols to serve the living and true God" (1:9). Recently I read an early Greek novel called *Anthia and Habrocomes*, and what stood out to me was this in-love-but-separated young couple were in two different exiles, and in each location they offered sacrifices to the gods and idols of each location. They didn't have one god or goddess; they worshiped whichever local god was wherever they were. Such was the Roman world. From such a way of life followers of Jesus converted. That conversion *from* was a conversion *to*, as well. They turned from false gods to the true God and to his Son who was coming back and who "rescues us from the coming wrath" (1:10). Wrath, which gets more attention in chapters four and five and then later in Paul's second letter to them, captures God's act of destroying evil and death in order to establish justice and the lordship of the world's one true Lord, Jesus.

Paul can't affirm the Thessalonians enough. So deep were their conversions in the crucible of suffering that they became a "model" for believers in the surrounding Macedonia and down the coast to Achaia, which means Philippi, Berea, Athens, and Corinth. They were Paul's success story. It's one thing to hear you are doing well in your music ministry or in your parenting or in the workplace, but it's another to say, "You have become the paradigm of what it means to do these things." Paul doesn't even have to tell those churches about the deep rootedness of the gospel among the Thessalonians. Word about them was suffusing like sunlight. Good followers of Jesus suffuse the light that way.

The tell-tale sign of a genuine conversion is when a person reworks their autobiography from "BC days" (Before Christ) to "AC days" (After Christ). That is, "I once was like that but now I'm different." Not long ago on a podcast I heard a well-known columnist say, "You can ask any of my friends. They'll all say I'm a different person. I'm not the person I was." That's conversion, and that's what Paul affirms about the Thessalonians. His words are a kind of "everybody's talking about you folks. And it's all good."

Words of affirmation carry deep value in the heart of those who are affirmed. Offer affirming words to your pastors about their ministries; to your neighbor about shoveling your snow when you were gone; about the beautiful personality of your spouse and your children; about the work a co-worker is doing. Figure out how you can affirm some fellow believers for their faith or love or hope, and maybe think about it through the terms Paul uses: work and labor and endurance.

QUESTIONS FOR REFLECTION AND APPLICATION

1. What does Paul affirm about the Thessalonians? How do you think these affirmations impacted them?

2. How did the Thessalonians serve as models for others in surrounding areas to imitate in the Christian life?

3. How does Paul use seemingly opposing terms together to create impact? What does he accomplish by pairing work/faith, labor/love, and endurance/hope?

4. Do you have any personal routines of prayer? How and when do you pray for others?

5. Who has affirmed you about your work, your labor, or your endurance? How did those affirmations affect you? Who will you affirm today about their example of faith, love, and hope?

FOR FURTHER READING

Scot McKnight, *The King Jesus Gospel: The Original Good News Revisited* (2d ed.; Grand Rapids: Zondervan, 2015).

REMEMBERING TIMES TOGETHER

1 Thessalonians 2:1–16

¹ You know, brothers and sisters, that our visit to you was not without results. ² We had previously suffered and been treated outrageously in Philippi, as you know, but with the help of our God we dared to tell you his gospel in the face of strong opposition. ³ For the appeal we make does not spring from error or impure motives, nor are we trying to trick you. ⁴ On the contrary, we speak as those approved by God to be entrusted with the gospel. We are not trying to please people but God, who tests our hearts. ⁵ You know we never used flattery, nor did we put on a mask to cover up greed—God is our witness. ⁶ We were not looking for praise from people, not from you or anyone else, even though as apostles of Christ we could have asserted our authority. ⁷ Instead, we were like young children among you.

Just as a nursing mother cares for her children, ⁸ so we cared for you. Because we loved you so much, we were delighted to share with you not only the gospel of God but our lives as well. ⁹ Surely you remember, brothers and sisters, our toil and hardship; we worked night and day in order not to be a burden to anyone while we preached the gospel of God to you. ¹⁰ You are witnesses, and so is God, of how holy, righteous and blameless we were among you who believed. *11* For you know that we dealt with each of you as a father deals with his own children, *12* encouraging, comforting and urging you to live lives worthy of God, who calls you into his kingdom and glory.

13 And we also thank God continually because, when you received the word of God, which you heard from us, you accepted it not as a human word, but as it actually is, the word of God, which is indeed at work in you who believe. *14* For you, brothers and sisters, became imitators of God's churches in Judea, which are in Christ Jesus: You suffered from your own people the same things those churches suffered from the Jews *15* who killed the Lord Jesus and the prophets and also drove us out. They displease God and are hostile to everyone *16* in their effort to keep us from speaking to the Gentiles so that they may be saved. In this way they always heap up their sins to the limit. The wrath of God has come upon them at last.

I like it when people of Kris's and my ages have a block of time to chat about the so-called 60s, which were actually far more the 70s. We each remember different items. We can talk Viet Nam and draft numbers, we can talk The Beatles and The Beach Boys and Jan and Dean (don't even say you've not heard of Jan and Dean) and Elvis. We can talk bell bottom jeans, love beads, head bands, skateboards, and our first summer jobs (baling hay and corn detassling). We can talk baseball going artificial turf, football creating a Super Bowl, and reading in school only white guys like Mark Twain and Ernest Hemingway. We remember how small most homes were, how big most cars were, how slow evenings on the porch without air conditioning were, and how few the options were on TV. Someone may mention Red Skelton and Carol Burnett and The Smothers Brothers. And go-go boots and Nancy Sinatra's famous "These Boots Are Made for Walking." And clothes designated for Sunday or very special events, like weddings and graduations and flying on an airplane. And teenagers with surfboards in swimming suits, all tanned up for the world ahead of them.

Remembering creates social bonds and common histories and identity-shaping events, and memories also give us courage and hope to carry on. More than once I've heard, "It was fun, but I'd never want to be that stupid again." Even more than that I've heard the soulful sounds of silent, sudden memories of times that made us who we are. It's good to explore the memories of common events. Not all memories are good. Some are painful, tear-shedding evocations of tragedies, like Kent State. Some bring to mind foolish decisions, morally sketchy moments, broken relationships, and bitter episodes of reactions and fights and arguments. Sometimes we remember when the whole world seemed against us and we had to find our own way. So we moved to another state, far away. We had to walk away from people and places and churches to start a new life.

Memories can be revealing. As Marilynne Robinson says in her wonderful novel *Gilead*, "Sometimes the visionary aspect of any particular day comes to you in the memory of it, or it opens to you over time. . . . I believe there are visions that come to us only in memory, in retrospect" (Robinson, *Gilead*, 91).

Paul remembers the good and difficult with the Thessalonians in our passage, and if you are alert to tone in what he writes you will also notice that he's defending himself against some accusations. It comes with the territory. To invade the space of others with the gospel may well provoke opposition and accusations, which at times will provoke explanation and defense.

Remembering Not Being Liked

Acts 17 tells us Paul opened his gospel campaign in Thessalonica in a synagogue. He reasoned with the leaders of that synagogue for three Sabbaths. He attempted to persuade them that Jesus was the Messiah and was the one crucified by the Roman authorities in a degrading, disgusting, barbaric act of cruelty used only for slaves. We forget how difficult it must have been even to get a decent conversation going. Some were persuaded, including Jews, god-fearing Greeks, and women (17:1–4).

Not all memories are about successful evangelistic events. Paul and Silas were the target of some opponents, but their opponents discovered the two gospelers were absent from the house church at Jason's, so the opponents nabbed him. Paul's opponents got one thing right. They knew his message was about "another king, one called Jesus" who was himself in some kind of opposition to Caesar (17:5–7). Jason posted bond and was released, and during the night, knowing danger lurked, they escorted Paul and Silas out of the city and sent them on their way (17:8–10). This is behind Paul's memories of being treated "outrageously in Philippi" (1 Thessalonians 2:2) and all this connects to facing "strong opposition" in Thessalonica.

We call what I just wrote "mirror reading," which describes reading, say a criticism by Paul as something being done by someone. Read 2:3–7 and think of Paul's claims as denials of criticisms lodged against him. My mirror reading yields at least the following bad memories for Paul: He was in "error" and had "impure motives" and was attempting to "trick" them, and he was not approved by God and was trying to "please people" and he used "flattery" and was greedy and wanted "praise from people" and was a bully who asserted his own "authority." Among the vices, flattery stands out because blarney was how many tried to butter others up. Paul and Silas and Timothy and all the co-workers experienced opposition in every city where they gospeled about Jesus. Some evening, sit down with your Bible and read 2 Corinthians 10–11 and do some mirror reading again. Your list of accusations against Paul will be long.

Sitting in a prison cell remembering all this with the Thessalonians may have been painful because these experiences were death-threatening and mission-risking moments when the gospel could have been stumped, suppressed, and stopped. So the leaders in that brand new church got together and said, "We gotta get this guy outta here." So they did. We read about this in Acts 17. Maybe Paul saw those early events in their city as an approach gone wrong. Maybe not. What he remembers for sure was that people just didn't like him. Ministry was hard.

REMEMBERING LOVING THEM AND BEING LOVED BY THEM

Paul flips images rather casually. He says in verse seven that "we were like young children among you" and in the second half of that verse he becomes a "nursing mother." He goes from being vulnerable, like children, to becoming responsible, like a mother. It's a daring image for a Jewish man. In Galatians 4:19 he gives birth, and in 1 Corinthians

113

3:1–2 he evokes breastfeeding (Gaventa, *Our Mother Saint Paul*). It was not unacceptable for Paul to talk like this, as can be seen in the prophet Isaiah 66:10–13. We find the same in the Dead Sea Scrolls (1QH 15.20–22): "You have made me a father for the sons of favor, like a wet-nurse . . . they open their mouth like a child." Still it was unusual to use such womanly images for himself.

His next step in remembering these very loving, intimate times is a kind of "remember when we were young and hung out in your backyard all summer long?" event. The term behind "our lives" is *psyche*, or our soul, our being, our deepest core. Again, notice that Paul's sense of teaching is not just words and ideas and propositions. He gives them words that are lived out in life itself; he gives them words that express who he is in his innermost being.

Paul remembers too how hard he and his companions were working for them–"night and day in order not to be a burden" (2:9). (Sing this to the tune "9 to 5" by Dolly Parton.) This points us to his manual labor day job so he could fund himself and his co-workers and not receive resources from them. Why? So he could not be accused of being a gospel huckster. Paul mentions this often. It's frequently missed so I recommend reading Acts 18:3, 2 Thessalonians 3:8–9, 1 Corinthians 9:6, 14; 2 Corinthians 11:7, 9, and 12:13. Not receiving money expressed his theory of ministry. His choice not to receive support both degraded his status in the Roman world while it also gave them an example of how to serve one another (Brookins, *1–2Thess*, 46–47). He didn't want to come off as a celebrity. He wanted to communicate that he was God's slave and their servant.

REMEMBERING TRUSTING

He asks them too to remember how "holy, righteous and blameless" he and his gospel workers were in those days (2:10). Image flip again: they were children, they were mothers, and now they are fathers! He was like a father (2:11) to them in this: "encouraging, comforting and urging you to live lives worthy of God" (2:12). That word "comforting" is picturesque: it evokes a parent *soothing* a crying, frustrated, or defeated child. Soothing removes heat from a situation.

When he gospeled in that synagogue some "received the word of God . . . not as a human word, but as . . . the word of God" (2:13). There are moments when God uses us to speak words that penetrate into a person's heart and mind as the very word of God. They trustingly listened and vulnerably received Paul's gospel as something from God, and everything changed for them from that day forward. Not only did they "receive" the gospel but the gospel about Jesus took over their lives.

REMEMBERING OPPOSITION TIMES

He's not done remembering with them because he knows the impact of their faith was that they became "imitators" of–a surprising new idea–"God's churches in Judea" (2:14). He now shifts from Thessalonica to Jerusalem, from opposition by synagogue leaders in Macedonia to Jerusalem's authorities. Paul recounts a historical reality next that has become a tragic memory for too many. Yes, Jesus was crucified and the authorities, both Roman and Jewish, played a part. Paul speaks of the latter as those "who killed the Lord Jesus" (2:15). The tragedy is that all Jews have at times been called "Christ killers" and have suffered immensely because of vicious and malicious Christian persecution. The Holocaust had more than one cause, but it was justified by some Christians by this very verse. So strong is the language of 2:15–16 that some scholars think these words were not from Paul but added by some scribe later (Gupta, *Critical Introduction*, 114–123, sketches the view and defends the words as Paul's).

Paul, like many of his contemporaries, both Jewish and gentile, is not above stereotyping with language, even using what we would call slander (Johnson, "The New Testament's Slander," 419-441). This is how ancients expressed fierce disagreement. That world is not ours, and such language about Jews became beyond dangerous once Christians got the upper hand in political, cultural, religious, and social power. "They displease God and are hostile to everyone" are yet more dangerous words. The hyperbole "hostile to everyone" permitted some Christians to turn all Jews into Christ-killing enemies. It's tragic. I lament the history and plead for you to use these words with the utmost of care. Yes, his concern crops up because of their opposition to his preaching to gentiles (2:16). But most don't hear that context. Most know the despicable brutality of the Crusades, and in medieval Europe Jews had to dress differently in order that others would know they weren't Christians. The Holocaust comes, and we are only beginning to escape the clutches of Christian bigotry. Paul remembered opposition, but we can learn to express our memories of such opposition in less offensive terms. Painful memories need not inflict pain on others.

QUESTIONS FOR REFLECTION
AND APPLICATION

1. What emotions do Paul's words here evoke in you? What emotions do Scot's memories of the 60s and 70s construct as you read them? How are they similar and different?

2. How does reading Acts alongside Paul's letters give additional insights into both texts? What are some ideas you have gleaned by trying this?

3. Where do you see Paul defending himself in this passage? Notice the "not . . . but" constructions or senses in 2:1–2, 3–4, 5, and 6–7 (Byron, *1–2Thess*, 59).

4. What impression do you get of Paul when he uses motherly imagery for himself and his ministry work?

5. Remember some of your highest and lowest ministry moments. How do those memories still impact you today?

FOR FURTHER READING

Beverly Gaventa, *Our Mother Saint Paul* (Louisville: Westminster John Knox, 2007).

Luke Timothy Johnson, "The New Testament's Slander and the Conventions of Ancient Polemic," *Journal of Biblical Literature* 108 (1989): 419–441.

Marilynne Robinson, *Gilead: A Novel* (New York: Farrar, Straus and Giroux, 2004).

ACHING FOR LIFE TOGETHER

1 Thessalonians 2:17–3:5

¹⁷ *But, brothers and sisters, when we were orphaned by being separated from you for a short time (in person, not in thought), out of our intense longing we made every effort to see you.* ¹⁸ *For we wanted to come to you—certainly I, Paul, did, again and again—but Satan blocked our way.* ¹⁹ *For what is our hope, our joy, or the crown in which we will glory in the presence of our Lord Jesus when he comes? Is it not you?* ²⁰ *Indeed, you are our glory and joy.*

^{3:1} *So when we could stand it no longer, we thought it best to be left by ourselves in Athens.* ² *We sent Timothy, who is our brother and co-worker in God's service in spreading the gospel of Christ, to strengthen and encourage you in your faith,* ³ *so that no one would be unsettled by these trials. For you know quite well that we are destined for them.* ⁴ *In fact, when we were with you, we kept telling you that we would be persecuted. And it turned out that way, as you well know.* ⁵ *For this reason, when I could stand it no longer, I sent to find out about your faith. I was afraid that in some way the tempter had tempted you and that our labors might have been in vain.*

At Northern Seminary some of our programs educate in the cohort model. Our New Testament cohorts begin the degree program together in a week-long intensive in late summer or early fall, and during each week we eat lunch together and become acquainted with one another enough to begin friendships. The rest of the school year students take classes together once a week in a hybrid classroom that combines some in-person students with some on Zoom. Rarely is the classroom just one cohort, which leads most of them to ache for the next intensive. Plans for the next cohort-only week start formulating—which restaurants, which evenings in Chicago. Sometimes on their Facebook cohort page someone expresses this: "I can't wait to be together!" Everyone clicks "Like."

Paul's aching for fellowship with the Thessalonians went to the next level.

ACHING FOR PRESENCE

He ached so much to be with them he said, "we were *orphaned* by being separated from you" (2:17 emphasis added). The NIV adds "by being separated" to clarify, but this reduces the emotional impact of Paul's terms (Gaventa, *1–2Thess*, 40). Being orphaned is more than being separated. Orphans lose (in that world) either of one's parents, and Paul turns the image upside down to point to losing one's children (Byron, *1–2Thess*, 93–94). Being orphaned is tragic, a profound loss, and the impacts can be devastating. His status as an orphan was forced upon him, as we read in Acts 17:10 that he and his co-workers had to be whisked away under the cover of darkness. Paul gives himself a variety of terms in our letter: mother, father, sibling, child, and orphan. Each of these family relationships morphed into an image for Paul to see himself.

He admits their separation was only "for a short time," but the ache was real. Notice other expressions of his aching heart: "out of our intense longing we made every effort to see you" and "we wanted to come to you" and he adds "again and again." He likes those people so much he says they are his hope and joy and crown (2:17–20).

Paul experienced roadblocks in wanting to return to visit with them, and he blames it on "Satan blocked our way" (2:18). In Acts 17's account of launching the gospel mission, we learn that the city's officials got involved enough to arrest Jason, which put Paul in jeopardy. Timothy Brookins wonders if the officials made an embargo against Paul, ordering him not to return (Brookins, *1–2Thess*, 67). That would have been a manifestation of Satan for Paul. *Anything* opposing the gospel work was the work of darkness, and Gaventa accurately describes Paul's experience as an "apocalyptic battle" (Gaventa, *1–2Thess*, 42).

To love someone is to be committed to being *with* them and to be *for* them so you can all grow together to be more like Christ. Some of our common life with one another is so close we can taste it and sense it and our bodies can ache for presence with one another. As David ached to be with Jonathan, as the exiles ached to return to Jerusalem to be with one another in the temple worshiping God, as the disciples ached to be with Jesus when they woke up to discover he had disappeared to a quiet place for prayer, and as Paul often ached to be with his co-workers–that's the ache at work in this passage. He pleads with Timothy, twice mind you, to get to Rome as fast as he can when Paul was in prison (2 Timothy 4:9, 21).

Perhaps some of us will have to think about Paul differently after pondering his ache to be with others. Some think Paul was a grumpy apostle running from city to city barking at bothersome Christians to get in line or else! I know at times I was tempted to think of him that way. Read 2 Corinthians 1–7 sometime and mark in your Bible his feelings and emotions. He was vulnerable to being accepted by others. He expressed his feelings without embarrassment; he told others about his emotions. Our passage is one of his vulnerable ones. He's probably in Corinth (after leaving Athens) and wants to see them; he's a long journey away and can't wait to be "on the road again."

ACHING'S SUBSTITUTE PRESENCE

But Paul won't be able to get on the road for awhile so he chooses second best: he sent Timothy (3:1–2, 5). No one could represent Paul better than Timothy, probably his closest co-worker. Timothy becomes Paul's surrogate or substitutionary presence (see Philippians 2:19).

How did Timothy get from Athens up to Thessalonica? Over three hundred miles. The planes and trains were on strike of course. So he had three ways to get there: by foot, by horse, by boat. Or combinations of each. Yes, that's how he got there. On a good day a healthy person can walk about 25 miles. There were stops and inns and tavernas along the way. Friends or family friends or connections here and there. But it's likely that it took more than two weeks for Timothy. And some time there. And two weeks more getting back. Sped up here and there if he could find a boat. Greeks have always loved boats.

While Timothy was traveling, Paul was waiting, and John Byron seems right to me when he says "his emotions and anxiety are getting the better of him" (Byron, *1–2Thess*, 96), and from the intensity of his language it does not look like he was a pro in patience. I once told a friend Kris and I had been to Australia. His quip reminds me of Paul. He said, "What I learned about that trip was that *When you think you can't stand the trip any longer you are about half way there!*" At least we knew how long our flight would last. Paul had no idea on how long it would be before he heard from Timothy.

ACHING'S PRESSING TOPIC

What was at the heart of Paul's aching to hear from them? Paul opens this topic for us by talking about their concern about *his* situation, only to leak information about his concern about *their* situation. He sends Timothy "to strengthen and encourage you in your faith" (3:2) because they are troubled over Paul's "trials" (3:3), a term that indicates pressure and persecution. He gives to them a theological explanation in the hope it will settle them: "you know quite well that we are destined for them" (3:3). In the top drawer of the 1st Century Jesus-follower's toolbox was the instruction that faithfulness in the way of Christ meant opposition, sometimes persecution, and sometimes martyrdom.

That Paul was experiencing persecution should not have surprised them. But when your teacher is put in prison for the gospel you begin to wonder if you might be next. The temptation to defect faces nearly everyone who undergoes persecution. Some people cave and squeal. Some run and hide. Some deny the faith. He doesn't want the Thessalonians to be "unsettled" by the stress that may come their way. He reminds them that the "we" he used in "we are destined for" persecution implies a "you too." Acts 17:6 is a clear case of opposing the gospel in this city, but in this letter itself we learn the Thessalonians themselves experienced some persecution. They responded to the gospel "in the midst of severe suffering" (1:6) and "you suffered from your own people" (2:14). Paul's concern was over their response to the persecutions.

This is why Paul sent Timothy, namely to find about their faith (3:5). This implies they, too, were facing stress for their allegiance to King Jesus. He was afraid, as he often was as a pastor in turbulent conditions, that the "tempter had tempted" them and that the work of Paul, Silas, and Timothy was wasted. Paul was anxious, and anxiety is a common human emotion about what one fears or expects. In anxiety the body goes into alert mode, and that mode was common for the apostle (2 Corinthians 11:28).

As Kellye Fabian Story, who was a serene presence in one of our Northern cohorts for four years, writes, anxiety reminds us of our "holy vulnerability." Paul's vulnerable anxiety prompted him to pray and talk with his companions and send letters and stand at the door and wait for Timothy to return with good news. To manage our anxieties, Kellye recommends from her own experience the following: surrender our bodies, pray common prayers, laugh out loud, encourage others, and the practice of eating together.

Managing anxiety is a Christian strategy; denouncing anxiety as sin is not. Aching for others we love will at times provoke a holy anxiety.

QUESTIONS FOR REFLECTION
AND APPLICATION

1. How does seeing the gentler side of Paul in passages like these impact your view of him?

2. What important roles does Timothy play in Paul's life and ministry?

3. What is the issue behind Paul's concern for the Thessalonians? What were the circumstances that made him feel anxious for them?

4. Have you experienced the ache of being separated from loved ones? How did that feel in your body? How do you relate with Paul here?

5. How do you manage your anxiety when worrying about people you love? What advice can you draw from Paul's example?

FOR FURTHER READING

Kellye Fabian, *Holy Vulnerability: Spiritual Practices for the Broken, Ashamed, Anxious, and Afraid* (Colorado Springs: NavPress, 2021).

THE JOY OF OTHERS LIKING YOU

1 Thessalonians 3:6–13

⁶ But Timothy has just now come to us from you and has brought good news about your faith and love. He has told us that you always have pleasant memories of us and that you long to see us, just as we also long to see you. ⁷ Therefore, brothers and sisters, in all our distress and persecution we were encouraged about you because of your faith. ⁸ For now we really live, since you are standing firm in the Lord. ⁹ How can we thank God enough for you in return for all the joy we have in the presence of our God because of you? ¹⁰ Night and day we pray most earnestly that we may see you again and supply what is lacking in your faith.

¹¹ Now may our God and Father himself and our Lord Jesus clear the way for us to come to you. ¹² May the Lord make your love increase and overflow for each other and for everyone else, just as ours does for you. ¹³ May he strengthen your hearts so that you will be blameless and holy in the presence of our God and Father when our Lord Jesus comes with all his holy ones.

What a relief! There's nothing like good news that relieves a person's ache and anxiety. It's like getting a "no cancer" report from the doctor's office when your biggest fear ransacked days of waiting. A giant sense of relief is what Paul felt when Timothy appeared on the horizon, and Michael Holmes is right when he says the relief seems "almost audible" (Holmes, *1–2Thess*, 99). We may hear Paul saying *Ahhhhhhhhh!* The previous passage (2:17–3:5) set us up for hearing that Timothy would inform Paul of the courage and faithfulness of the Thessalonians. But Paul throws a curve ball in our passage before he tosses what we expect.

THEIR LOVE FOR PAUL

Yes, we will hear about their faithfulness next, but before Paul gets there he goes off the charts with joy because–wait for it–they like him! They "always have pleasant memories," or "good memories," about Paul, Silas, and Timothy. They "long to see" them (3:6). This very passage reminds me of Paul's lack of peace when in Troas, hoping to meet up with his other ambassador, Titus. He wanted good news from Corinth. No Titus, so Paul moved on (2 Corinthians 2:5–13). Only five chapters later do we get that meeting and Paul explodes into joy there too (7:5–7). Paul's anxiety was relieved when he learned his churches loved him!

Relief comes through Paul's circle in all sorts of "distress and persecution" (3:7). The good news from Timothy lifted them out of their nasty circumstances into the joy of the Lord. Ministry for Paul was as much *personal* as it was professional, pastoral, and theological. He loved these people, and what they thought of him mattered to him. We all could write some notes or express our love for and give affirmations to those who serve us. If we are ministering to others, we can set an example by offering words of gratitude ourselves–which often unleash a cycle of encouragements.

What brought joy to Paul was their "faith and love" (3:6), beginning with their love and then turning to their faith.

THEIR FIRM FAITH

We expect to hear something about their rock-solid faithfulness, and it comes when Paul speaks of their "faith" (3:6, 7) and their "standing firm in the Lord" (3:8). The word "faith" has three elements in the New Testament: it means the initial act of trusting in Jesus as God's Messiah, Savior, and Lord; it means allegiance or faithfulness or trust over the long haul; and it means The Faith, that is, what we believe to be true as Christians (Bates, *Gospel Allegiance*).

The NIV translates "standing firm" though the Greek text really only has "standing." The idea is standing, not being blown down by the winds of the evil one, and not being knocked over by the pressure of their "own people" (2:14; cf. 1:6). Paul not only likes being liked by them, but he is profoundly joyous over their faithfulness. Together these feelings turn into a summary expression: "Now we really live" (3:8). The audible relief of *Ahhhhhhh* again. Life comes to life for him because he has heard from Timothy that they're hanging on and holding out for the gospel about Jesus. It sounds weird, but Paul was made for this church-planting mission and the discipleship mentoring that followed. In every city the church was an upstart movement, and regressing or returning to their former ways of life were much easier than associating with a group of Roman discontents who now think a crucified Jew is the

Jewish Messiah. They no doubt had heard this one: "How can you believe a crucified man, which is the ultimate degradation reserved only for slaves, is the Lord of the Realm and the world's true king? It makes no sense." That they stood firm "in the Lord" sent Paul over the moon.

THEIR PRAYER

You will be forgiven if you think Paul's about to close this letter because he often prays at the end of a letter. It's not the end of the letter, however much it may feel like it. The elements of his prayer are:

> For his return to Thessalonica (3:10, 11), and it has been 6–12 months.
> For their love to "increase and overflow for each other and for everyone else" (3:12).
> For God to "strengthen your hearts" so at the Second Coming they will be found "blameless and holy" (3:13).

His concerns remain constant: he wants to be with them because he loves them; he wants them to grow in love for one another; and he wants them to experience the spiritual formation that yields allegiance so they will be found worthy of the Lord at his coming.

Beginnings of letters and ends of letters often express similar themes, and if you look back to 1:2–3 you will see what I mean. There Paul thanked God for their faith, their love, and their hope. In 3:6 he hears about their faith and love, and in 3:9–10 he prays for their faith to grow and in 3:12 he prays for their love to flourish and in 3:13 it appears he prays for their hope to intensify. Paul was the kind of person who wrote in order to discover what he was actually thinking. R. Scott Brunner, in his wonderful little book *Due South*, once asked, "How do I know what I think until I have written about it?" Thinking his way forward, Paul writes up his prayer and, as he prays, he realizes he's got more to say, which is why we have chapters four and five!

This passage completes the story of Paul's relationship with the Thessalonians. He will turn in chapter four to the moral vision he has for them before he deals with two questions about the Second Coming that Timothy must have said were percolating in every home study group in Thessalonica.

Questions for Reflection and Application

1. What clues do you see in this letter that ministry is deeply personal for Paul?

2. How can Paul's prayer here guide you into new insights about prayer? What can you learn from imitating his example?

3. What are the three elements of "faith" in the New Testament?

4. In your own ministry experiences, how have you dealt with the issue of whether or not people like you? When have you felt insecurity or relief and reassurance?

5. Take time to celebrate the faith, hope, and love of Christians you have discipled, mentored, or cared for. What do you want to pray for them?

FOR FURTHER READING

Matthew Bates, *Gospel Allegiance* (Grand Rapids: Brazos, 2019).
R. Scott Brunner, *Due South: Dispatches from Down Home* (New York: Villard, 2001).

A LIFE THAT PLEASES GOD

1 Thessalonians 4:1–12

¹ As for other matters, brothers and sisters, we instructed you how to live in order to please God, as in fact you are living. Now we ask you and urge you in the Lord Jesus to do this more and more. ² For you know what instructions we gave you by the authority of the Lord Jesus.

³ It is God's will that you should be sanctified: that you should avoid sexual immorality; ⁴ that each of you should learn to control your own body in a way that is holy and honorable, ⁵ not in passionate lust like the pagans, who do not know God; ⁶ and that in this matter no one should wrong or take advantage of a brother or sister. The Lord will punish all those who commit such sins, as we told you and warned you before. ⁷ For God did not call us to be impure, but to live a holy life. ⁸ Therefore, anyone who rejects this instruction does not reject a human being but God, the very God who gives you his Holy Spirit.

⁹ Now about your love for one another we do not need to write to you, for you yourselves have been taught by God to love each other. ¹⁰ And in fact, you do love all of God's family throughout Macedonia. Yet we urge you, brothers and sisters, to do so more and more, ¹¹ and to make it your ambition to lead a quiet life: You

should mind your own business and work with your hands, just as we told you, [12] so that your daily life may win the respect of outsiders and so that you will not be dependent on anybody.

In the Bible there are a few basic, or major, approaches to summarizing how we are to live before God, or what we might call "Summaries of the Christian life." One can summarize the law of Moses, or one can turn to the wisdom teachings of Proverbs, or to the big themes of the prophets, like justice and peace and economic equity. When we turn to the New Testament we can begin with Jesus' teachings, summarized as they are in the Sermon on the Mount, or we can turn to life in the Spirit in Paul's letters, or the apostle John's walking in love and light in 1 John, or to James' wisdom teachings, or to Hebrews (at times a bit) fierce warnings about faithfulness. And then there's the Book of Revelation.

Each has its own approach to the Christian life, but they all overlap into a sizable Venn diagram. And Paul himself can summarize the Christian life in a number of ways. Our passage is one of those. In light of what has just been said, we are wise to listen carefully to each of them, to learn from each, but without exaggerating any of them into the Be-All and End-All way of talking about the Christian life. For the Thessalonians, Paul thought it best to speak of one big category (pleasing God) with three components (holiness/sanctification, love, and a quiet life).

PLEASING GOD

Paul taught them already about pleasing God (4:2; cf. 4:6, 11), and what he taught the Thessalonians accepted (4:1).

He now both asks them and urges them to "live" that way and "to do this more and more." There is a pastoral softening here worth pausing to consider. Paul bounces "ask" and "urge" (or "encourage" in a comforting manner) off one another. By doing this the "urge" is not as forceful, and their will or agency are engaged to make daily decisions ("more and more") about pleasing God. In fact, "more and more" translates a verb that suggests abounding. That's his desire–that they flourish in pleasing God.

He repeats that they know this already, which is a clever way of saying *Pleasing God is not new teaching.* In 4:2 he speaks of "instructions," better translated "encouragement," that they taught the Thessalonians way back when they launched the church. He encouraged them "through the Lord," the NIV making it a bit more specific with "*by the authority of* the Lord Jesus." It's important for him that he is not laying down new rules and regs. No, he's passing on what life looks like in and through the Lord Jesus in the power of the Spirit (Gaventa, *1–2Thess*, 49).

Pleasing God, a core idea for Christian ethics, is the appropriate response to a covenant relationship to the Father through Jesus in the power of the Spirit. As the Father was "well pleased" with the Son (Matthew 3:17) so we can experience the Father's pleasure in us and our pleasure in God. To please God is about relational connection.

Loving and pleasing God form into the major idea in our passage, and Paul breaks them down into three components, the first one getting the most attention.

Please God with Holiness

The Thessalonians are to please God by being holy in their sexual behaviors. Paul writes, God's "will" is "that you should be sanctified," or "your holiness" (4:3). So commonly do preachers and teachers say that holiness means separation from what is common or sinful that we are caught in this web of meaning. However, the term holiness points first to the *presence of God in Christ*, and second to *devotion or dedication to Christ* and, because someone is dedicated to God, that person is only their *withdrawn from common, sinful living* (separate). To speak only of separation is to lose the meaning of the term by more than half. Paul then is not saying *God wants you to withdraw from worldliness* so much as *God wants you to be in the presence of Christ by being devoted to him, and therefore to stay away from sinfulness.*

Paul's two first-day-of-discipleship-class instructions for gentile converts were:

1. Put idols behind them
2. To avoid sexual sins

Our world does not take the first literally very often, though one sometimes hears about the idolatry of greed and consumerism and violence and war and even guns. Paul, however, was talking about gentile religions and physical idols, the latter found in most homes on an altar. But he named the sins and was unafraid to use strong language. As Dietrich Bonhoeffer once said, "A church-community which does not call sin sin will likewise be unable to find faith when it wants to grant forgiveness of sin" (Bonhoeffer, *Discipleship*, 262). But Paul does not name people to crush them. "Certainly, it is because of our sin that we must be spoken to in such a harsh language; but we are being spoken to, not destroyed." So said Alan Jacobs in his essay volume *Shaming the Devil* (p. 69).

In that context the concern was sexual sins, so he said to "avoid sexual immorality." The expression "sexual immorality" could be translated "prostitution," which was more common in that world than it is now. Here's a summary of sexual life in the Jewish stereotype of gentile men in two observations: first, sexual penetration meant domination. Thus, the former person was superior to the latter person. Second, in the Roman world males had sex at home with one's wife and outside (or at times inside) the home with slaves and prostitutes. Such is of course a stereotype that works because it fits some realities, but not all. That stereotype was used both by Jews and gentiles (Byron, *1–2Thess*, 130). We should not exaggerate either gentile sinfulness or Jewish, Christian uniqueness. But neither should we pretend to their being alike in sexual ethics. The Christian teaching on sexual purity, which was fidelity to one's spouse, was a thick, high wall many early male converts had to scale if they wanted to live with holiness in the community of faith.

Paul explains how devotion to God and sexual purity work themselves out. First, that a person is to "control" or even "acquire" in the sense of taking responsibility for and control of "your own body." The term "body" here translates to "vessel" in the KJV. Who or what is this "vessel"? One's wife? (Notice 1 Peter 3:7.) One's sexual organ? (Notice 1 Samuel 21:5.) Or one's own body? Probably the latter as the NIV has it. Second, this kind of self-discipline, which differed dramatically from the indulgences of the Roman and Greek worlds, turned away from the "passionate lust" of the "pagans" (4:5). Again, he's speaking of the proliferation of sexual promiscuity of the gentile world, something Jews criticized constantly because, like Paul, he knew they did "not know God" (4:5).

Paul's third explanation is not entirely clear: "in this matter no one should wrong or take advantage of a brother" (and the NIV adds "or sister")(4:6). I'll tell you what I think. Paul is telling a man not to step over the line to engage in sexual relations with another man's household member. As already stated, gentile sexual boundaries were wide while Jewish and Christian boundaries were much tighter. Christian sexual ethics began at ground zero in Thessalonica so such a reading would make sense to them. They had to learn a new way of life daily because their fleshly habits were the product of a life of bad decisions. Willa Cather put a warning to all of us in a musing of one of her characters when she wrote, "The first time I deceived my grandparents I felt rather shabby, perhaps even the second time, but I soon ceased to think about it" (Cather, *My Ántonia*, 165).

Paul warns them of God's judgment (4:6) because God has called the church to "live a holy life" (4:7). With "impure," Paul evokes the catalogue of sexual sins in Leviticus 18. Succumbing to this most common temptation was, Paul says severely, rejecting God, the God who has filled them with the Spirit who can transform them into a holy way of life, which pleases God.

PLEASE GOD WITH LOVE FOR ONE ANOTHER

A second component of pleasing God is to love one another. Paul has mentioned love (*agape*) already (1:3; 36, 12) and will raise it again (5:8, 13), but Paul changes terms in 4:9 to *philadelphia*, which in Paul's letters means "sibling-love," love for fellow believers as brothers and sisters. In the span of a few words, he says they have already "been taught by God to love [*agape*] each other" (4:9). To love is to make a rugged, affective commitment to another person in being present with them, in being for them as an advocate, all to grow together in walking in a way that pleases God. The "mark" of the Christian, Francis Schaeffer once scolded the evangelical world in a powerful way, was to love one another as Jesus taught us to love (John 13; Schaeffer, *The Mark of a Christian*).

It didn't take long before the local churches became the universal church. The Thessalonians have extended their sibling-love/*agapē* love to "all of God's family throughout Macedonia" (4:10), and Paul wants that kind of love to flourish like wrapped gifts at Christmas. Sibling-love among Christians created a widespread network of hospitality for traveling Christians, as it also turned a strange city into new sibling relations (Pohl, *Making Room*). That is, each city had an open Airbnb for Christians on the road.

PLEASE GOD WITH A QUIET LIFE

Two down, one to go. The third component of pleasing God is to live, or love, the honor of a "quiet life" (4:11), which means (1) minding your own business and (2) working one's own hands. The aim of this kind of quiet working life is to "win the respect of outsiders," and to avoid taxing or exploiting Christian hospitality by not being "dependent on anybody" (4:12). The theme of forming a good reputation is found in both 1 Peter 2:10–3:7 but also throughout 1–2 Timothy and Titus. Minority groups can establish themselves as safe and not disruptive by becoming good people with socially respectable conduct.

That Paul has to tell them to be quiet and to work with their own hands probably indicates some had stopped working because they thought Jesus was about to return. Notice that 5:13–14, which says much the same as 4:11–12, both surround two passages about the Second Coming. Others think these teachings are more about urging the Christians to become more self-dependent, which is a typical reading of the same theme in 2 Thessalonians 3:6–13.

Let's not forget the big picture: the emphasis here falls on three components of one big idea–pleasing God:

> By sexual holiness that takes its cues from
> God's will,
> by loving one another,
> and by conducting their public life in a quiet,
> respectable manner.

QUESTIONS FOR REFLECTION AND APPLICATION

1. How does Paul approach teaching the Thessalonians to live a life that pleases God? What is his strategy and his overall message?

2. What does Paul teach them about pleasing God through their holiness?

3. How were the Thessalonians to please God through their sibling love for one another?

4. What are the elements here of a "quiet life" that pleases God?

5. When you think about your own approach to interpreting the Bible to guide you into a life that pleases God, which approach do you tend to focus on? The teachings of Moses, the wisdom of the Proverbs, the social justice of the prophets, the sermons of Jesus, the letters of Paul, or something else?

FOR FURTHER READING

Dietrich Bonhoeffer, *Discipleship* (Minneapolis: Fortress, 2001).

Willa Cather, *My Ántonia* (New York: Farrar, Straus and Giroux, 1996).

Alan Jacobs, *Shaming the Devil: Essays in Truthtelling* (Grand Rapids: Wm. B. Eerdmans, 2004).

Christine D. Pohl, *Making Room: Recovering Hospitality as a Christian Tradition* (Grand Rapids: Wm. B. Eerdmans, 1999).

Francis Schaeffer, *The Mark of a Christian* (2d. ed.; Downers Grove, Ill.: IVP Books, 2006).

A QUESTION ABOUT THOSE WHO DIE

1 Thessalonians 4:13–18

[13] Brothers and sisters, we do not want you to be uninformed about those who sleep in death, so that you do not grieve like the rest of mankind, who have no hope. [14] For we believe that Jesus died and rose again, and so we believe that God will bring with Jesus those who have fallen asleep in him. [15] According to the Lord's word, we tell you that we who are still alive, who are left until the coming of the Lord, will certainly not precede those who have fallen asleep. [16] For the Lord himself will come down from heaven, with a loud command, with the voice of the archangel and with the trumpet call of God, and the dead in Christ will rise first. [17] After that, we who are still alive and are left will be caught up together with them in the clouds to meet the Lord in the air. And so we will be with the Lord forever. [18] Therefore encourage one another with these words.

There are very few topics that generate more questions than when someone begins teaching about the future—about the Second Coming or the Rapture or the Tribulation or the Millennium. Many of these questions get specific, like, Do you think so-and-so is the Antichrist? Do you think the European Union is predicted in Revelation? Do you think the Tribulation is about to begin? When I was in college, I heard someone say Mikhail Gorbachev was the antichrist, and why not with that birthmark on his head? So, questions about questions folded over more questions.

Our passage above is the famous "rapture" passage. In fact, the only passage in the whole Bible that *could* be read as one that teaches (1) a resurrection of those "dead in Christ," (2) a snatching up into the air of those Christians still alive when Jesus descends and (3) the snatched or raptured are held in the sky until the Great Tribulation is over when the same persons return to the earth for a 1000 year millennium. We can presume the dead and the alive are both raptured. There are three problems with this common reading. First, this is the only passage that teaches a rapture the way many think of it, and one can wonder why a rapture never occurs in Jesus' own predictions of the future (say Mark 13) or in the book of books about the future, namely, the Book of Revelation. One can also wonder why Paul never brings this up again in his other letters. Which leads many, second, to think this passage is not actually teaching a rapture like that at all. Instead, they think vv. 16–17 are metaphors drawn from the customary way Roman leaders left the city to meet with dignitaries outside the city when they were arriving. A kind of "we will all go meet the Lord when he comes and then go to heaven" idea. Third, the most important part of this passage gets mostly, if not entirely, ignored when we get caught up in rapture speculations. What matters most both begins the passage (4:13) and ends it (4:18; note 5:11, too), and I will do the same here.

Encourage One Another

Some new believers were so convinced of the imminent return of Jesus (the Second Coming) that they were scandalized by the deaths of believers. They were evidently grieving intensely "like the rest of mankind" (better, "the rest" or "the remaining" of people) who "have no hope" (4:13). Instead of finding deep consolation in God's promised future, they were overwhelmed with thoughts of the dead in grimy darkness or suffering or isolation, and then perhaps of never seeing them again. Or perhaps they were saddened over a soul being separated forever from a recognizable body. Perhaps they were wondering if death was the final word. Paul wanted them to know death was not the final word and that such a grieving without hope was not the way of the Christian. Life was the final word for them, and with life comes hope.

So Paul says "Therefore encourage one another" (4:18). Come alongside them, perhaps give them a hug or a side hug or a hand on the shoulder or look them in the eyes and speak the word that life is the last word. One of those words is that for believers death is a kind of *sleeping* from which one wakes up (4:13, 14, 15). Belief in resurrection turns death into sleep. Believers are surely sad over the deaths of family and friends but they can "grieve with hope" (Byron, *1–2Thess*, 154).

Here's the reason we begin with "encourage one another": the intent of this passage is to encourage the living believers that their dead-in-Christ siblings are not extinguished but will be raised to be with the Lord and with them. Death is not the final word; life is. Whatever those difficult rapture-like verses mean, they're here as a way of encouraging believers they will all be gathered together with Jesus.

RE-THINKING RAPTURE

If we are going to reconsider how many think about rapture, the first word to think about is "resurrection" because Jesus "died and rose again" (4:14). No resurrection, no hope. Resurrection means hope for those in Christ. That's encouraging.

Then Paul says, "God will *bring* with Jesus" (4:14), and that little word "bring" translates a word so common it has thirty-eight different senses in my Greek lexicon! The sense in our passage is "take" (not "bring" as in the NIV) and here's why: this little word is clarified by what Jesus does in verses sixteen and seventeen. Jesus will descend, the archangel's and the Lord's voice will be heard, the dead will be raised to be with Jesus, and the living believers will join the dead to be with Jesus forever. Thus, the sense of the term "bring" is to "gather people to a returning Jesus" to be with him, which too is encouraging.

Now what about "caught up together with them" (4:17)? The oddity here is that some believe in a kind of sky box theory. That is, some think these saints will be raptured to Jesus in the sky and, still in the sky, they will be seated in the front row for the entire tribulation watching the judgments of God unfurled on earth . . . and, frankly, this doesn't strike many as realistic. This text, instead, refers to a translation or assumption or lifting into heaven. That's it. The term "coming" of the Lord in 4:15 (*parousia*) was often used for a Roman emperor arriving at a city. Plus, the word Paul uses for "to meet" is the very term used frequently in Jewish and Greek texts for dignitaries in a city departing from the city to meet with arriving emperors and ambassadors. When they meet they exchange greetings and kisses and welcomes, and only then turn around to enter into the city with fanfare. Jesus used the term that way (Matthew 25:6; Sidebar). Notice that whereas human dignitaries met on the road outside the city as a show of their power in the territory, Jesus is met in the air because he is the Lord over "all territories" (Gaventa, *1–2Thess*, 66). Many today prefer this metaphorical sense of "rapture/meet" rather than a physical sense. I do, too. That we could be caught up to be with Jesus is encouraging, too.

Rapture or not, the passage sketches two major themes about the future: One, that Jesus will come again, and two, that believers will be united with him to spend eternity with him and with one another.

ENCOURAGE AGAIN

What we can all agree on is that Life, not death, has the final word. Amidst the grief at a funeral can be the celebration of endless life with the Lord Jesus, whether it happens in the ordinary form of dying or in the extraordinary form of a future translation to heaven to be with Jesus at the Second Coming. The passage begins and then ends on a note of encouragement because knowing these two major themes is a source of consolation in the face of loved ones dying: "Therefore encourage one another with these words" (4:18). Tom Wright offers these words of encouragement in light of what this passage is about–victory over death: "One day all creation will be rescued from slavery, from the corruption, decay, and death which deface its beauty, destroy its relationships, remove the sense of God's presence from it, and make it a place of injustice, violence, and brutality" (Wright, *Simply Christian*, 126).

Jesus: "At midnight the cry rang out: 'Here's the bridegroom! Come out *to meet him!*'" (Matthew 25:6).

For Paul: "The brothers and sisters there had heard that we were coming, and they traveled as far as the Forum of Appius and the Three Taverns *to meet us.* At the sight of these people Paul thanked God and was encouraged" (Acts 28:15).

When Joseph understood that his father was coming, for Judas his brother was come before him, and informed him of his approach, he went out *to meet him*; and they met together at Heliopolis (Josephus, *Antiquities* 2.184 [2.7.5]).

When Jonathan therefore had overcome so great an army, he removed from Ashdod, and came to Askelon; and when he had pitched his camp without the city, the people of Askelon *came out and met him*, bringing him hospitable presents, and honoring him; so he accepted of their kind intentions, and returned thence to Jerusalem with a great deal of prey, which he brought thence when he conquered his enemies (Josephus, *Antiquities* 13.101 [13.4.4]).

Now Antonius and Caesar had beaten Cassius near Philippi, as others have related; but after the victory, Caesar went into Gaul [Italy], and Antony marched for Asia, who when he was arrived at Bithynia, he had ambassadors *that met him* from all parts (Josephus, *Antiquities* 14.301 [14.12.2]).

QUESTIONS FOR REFLECTION AND APPLICATION

1. What have you been taught or read about the end times and the rapture? How does the approach here differ from or confirm your previous ideas?

2. How does Paul use hope and encouragement in his teachings about death and the future?

3. What are some of the possible interpretations of this passage regarding how Jesus will come back to meet us?

4. Think of phrases other Christians have said to you when you lost a loved one. Which were encouraging? Which were not? What would you most want to hear from Christian leaders when you are grieving?

5. How will you pass on Paul's hope about resurrection and life to others who are grieving?

FOR FURTHER READING

N.T. Wright, *Simply Christian: Why Christianity Makes Sense* (New York: HarperOne, 2010).

A QUESTION ABOUT TIMES AND DATES

1 Thessalonians 5:1–11

[1] *Now, brothers and sisters, about times and dates we do not need to write to you,* [2] *for you know very well that the day of the Lord will come like a thief in the night.* [3] *While people are saying, "Peace and safety," destruction will come on them suddenly, as labor pains on a pregnant woman, and they will not escape.*

[4] *But you, brothers and sisters, are not in darkness so that this day should surprise you like a thief.* [5] *You are all children of the light and children of the day. We do not belong to the night or to the darkness.* [6] *So then, let us not be like others, who are asleep, but let us be awake and sober.* [7] *For those who sleep, sleep at night, and those who get drunk, get drunk at night.* [8] *But since we belong to the day, let us be sober, putting on faith and love as a breastplate, and the hope of salvation as a helmet.* [9] *For God did not appoint us to suffer wrath but to receive salvation through our Lord Jesus Christ.* [10] *He died for us so that, whether we are awake or asleep, we may live together with him.* [11] *Therefore encourage one another and build each other up, just as in fact you are doing.*

Another question about the future arose among the Thessalonians, and it's one I've heard asked hundreds of times in my own life. Along the lines of the previous passage, though now shifting from the dead to the living (Byron, *1–2Thess*, 163–164), our passage responds to questions the Thessalonians are asking about the "day of the Lord" (5:2). This time they want to know "times and dates" (5:1), that is, they are wondering if Paul also has a time schedule. As a college student I thought I had all this figured out because I had read the latest and freshest predictions of when the rapture would happen. While a teen I heard a convincing sermon that Jesus *had to return by 1975*! In a bookstore with a Calvin seminary student I struck up a conversation, which led to my fascination with the rapture. I asked him what he believed and when he thought it would occur. His words have stayed with me: "I don't know when our Lord will return. But I do know this: It could be soon, and I must be ready." For Paul the *When* question was not remotely as important as the *How to Live* question. It is unfortunate that so many get entangled in predictions that are proven wrong and so distort the intent of words like those in our passage. The most accurate title for a series on the future would be "We're Still Here (so let's live faithfully in hope)!"

This readiness pertains to what can best be called an "interim" between the times, between the first and second coming of Christ. In this period we live in the present world with its limitation in light of the future world with its perfections and glories. We live in the Now *as if* it were Then. Yet there is to be a kind of discontent with the Now because of what we know about the Then. It's a bit like a young teacher being a substitute until an opportunity to be a full-time teacher arrives, or like a talented basketball player playing in the NCAA knowing she will be drafted in the WNBA. Life in the Now is the staging ground for the full form of the kingdom. Maybe we should show some sympathy to those early Christians. Many of them knew their Bibles and the hopes and expectations associated with the arrival of the Messiah. Perhaps they were saying, "Jesus is surely the Messiah, but are these conditions of life all we get out of all those glorious promises? When's the fullness arriving? How soon is it?" Paul's words, Beverly Gaventa reminds us, about the Parousia "may be trusted, but it cannot be predicted" (Gaventa, *1–2Thess*, 68).

Let us offer one word of counsel for pondering passages like this one, that is, eschatological passages. Keep the big picture in mind: God will conquer evil and erase it from history so God's people can live in peace, justice, and love. Speculations about who and when and who will do what distract us from the big picture.

A TIME THAT WILL SURPRISE

In the previous passage we read about the "coming of the Lord" (4:15), or the *Parousia* (appearing, manifestation of the Lord) but in our new passage the question is about the "day of the Lord" (5:2). Are these two expressions pointing us to the same event in history? As Jeffrey Weima puts it, in the Old Testament (Isaiah 2:12; Amos 5:18–20) the very common expression, the "day" of the Lord, "refers to a future time when God would come both to punish the wicked and to vindicate his people," and he is accurate also in saying the emphasis of such a day is much more judgment than deliverance (Weima, *1–2Thess*, 346). The early Christians very simply translated "day of the Lord" into the (second) "coming of Christ" (1 Thessalonians 5:4; Romans 2:5). Paul uses "day of the Lord" here instead of the "coming" (4:15) because his emphasis is on God's swift judgment ("destruction" at 5:3 and "wrath" at 5:9). These two expressions–day of the Lord, coming of Christ–point us to the same general event of judgment and redemption.

Jesus didn't know when that day would happen (Mark 13:32), Paul didn't know, and so the Thessalonians' question was unanswerable. In fact, he says "you know" *accurately* or even *precisely*, which are better translations than "very well" (NIV; 5:2). They have been taught and know with precision the answer to the question they ask. But he clarifies with a mixture of images. It will be like a "thief in the night" (Matthew 24:42–44), or when people think all is well and there is, like the *Pax Romana*, an abundance of "peace and safety," the Lord will come "suddenly" as do the "labor pains" arrive for "a pregnant woman" (1 Thessalonians 5:2–3). Capturing more of the night image, he says the believers are not in the "darkness" or the "night," and the latter was far darker for them than it is for us. By association, it is at night when people are "asleep" or "drunk" (5:4, 5, 6, 7).

In the interim they live not knowing *when*, but they know what the End will bring. So, they must be ready.

A TIME TO BE READY

To help them understand what it means to be ready, Paul again trades in two images–to be people of the "light" and the "day" and to be "awake and sober" (5:5, 6, 8). People sleep at night; people get drunk in the dark. These are his images for moral unpreparedness. Sleepiness and stupors do not permit ready responses. But moral preparedness means being awake and sober by living in the "light" of the "day," which are times for most people to be alert and ready to work.

Images work when they give us new ways to think about being ready. Alertness for the coming of Christ means faithfulness, obedience, and moral responsibility. So Paul turns daylight living into his three favorite Christian virtues: faith, love, and hope. Those words are how one becomes ready for the return of Christ. Faith and faithfulness are joined at the hip as a life of ongoing trust in the Lord. Love points us to the Jesus Creed of loving God and loving others as ourselves (Mark 12:29–31; see Galatians 5:13–14), and hope is a life of faith that is shaped toward knowing the promises of God will come true: justice and peace will be the only way of life because injustice and war will be doomed to extinction.

The battle for readiness requires military gear (cf. Ephesians 6:10–17). Paul attaches a military image to each of these virtues: faith and love are the breastplate, which indicates torso protection against the powers of this world like systemic injustices, the powers of darkness, and the habits of the flesh. Hope is attached to "salvation" as the future completion of God's work in the New Jerusalem, and it is the "helmet," which obviously protects the head (5:8). Seeing a breastplate and helmet as protections of the heart and mind is no stretch of the imagination.

A TIME OF HOPE

In the interim between the first and second comings, believers are to be shaped by hope instead of despair and fleshly indulgences. Their future is "salvation" (5:9). Salvation in the New Testament has three tenses: we have been saved (past), we are now working out salvation (present), and the final completion of salvation is future. In 5:9 salvation is future, and it is spelled out as a life "together with" Jesus (5:10). Our future presence with him is secured because Jesus has "died for us," and this expression requires that we connect his death to the next term. We are not appointed by God "to suffer wrath" because Jesus has died to remedy us so that God's wrath against sin, flesh, the devil, and systemic injustice does not come our way. His resurrection broke the powers of the death he died and so secures our resurrection. As John Byron points out, God's wrath in the Old Testament is not about God's vindictiveness but his moral outrage against human oppression of the poor (Isaiah 10:1–6), ignoring widows and orphans (Zechariah 7:9–12), and meting out injustices (Isaiah 5:21–25) (Byron, *1–2Thess*, 171). The return of Christ is a time when God routs the ways of systemic injustices and sin.

We need to remind ourselves perhaps of something. So much of heaven talk is about what we *get* when we get there—gold and food and happiness and festive occasions. What we get is small potatoes to *who we will be with*. To be with Jesus, to be with God, to bask in God's glory and the presence of others are what matter most. Getting is nothing compared to gathering.

A TIME OF SUPPORTING ONE ANOTHER

In the midst of a Roman world shaped by completely different moral categories and by various idolatries, to walk in the way of Jesus could be very lonely. And scary and stressful. But the believer is not alone. So Paul reminds them of what he had written at the end of the previous passage

(4:18) to "encourage one another and build each other up" (5:11). Passages about the future are not threats; they are moral exhortations that are shaped to encourage us. The Thessalonians are, Paul knows, already "doing" this but he wants them to continue. A life of faith, love, and hope is not accomplished by a single decision or a one-time action. It is as daily as walking and working and living.

I find encouragement in these words by my colleague, Beth Felker Jones: "When death is finally no more, we will be shaped entirely by the love embodied in Jesus Christ. Finally, our bodies are for praise, praise of the one who is victor over death, who will shape us into witnesses to beauty, to goodness, to holiness, and to peace" (*Marks of His Wounds*, 112). Forever and ever we will be intoxicated with God's glorious presence, and that presence will lead us ever onwards into the pleasures of beauty and holiness and peace. That vision encourages and prompts me to live like that now (as much as possible).

QUESTIONS FOR REFLECTION AND APPLICATION

1. What is the big picture idea about the future we should keep in mind?

2. How can Christians get themselves ready for Jesus to return?

3. What is the biblical evolution of "day of the Lord" to "coming of Christ"? Why does Paul use "day of the Lord"?

4. How does Paul's vision for the future encourage you to live faithfully today?

5. As you consider a heavenly future, what most excites you about it?

FOR FURTHER READING

Beth Felker Jones, *Marks of His Wounds: Gender Politics and Bodily Resurrection* (New York: Oxford University Press, 2007).

SYSTEMIC, SYSTEMIC

1 Thessalonians 5:12–28 (reformatted)

^{12} *Now we ask you, brothers and sisters, [1a] to acknowledge those who work hard among you, who care for you in the Lord and who admonish you.* ^{13} *[1b] Hold them in the highest regard in love because of their work.*

[2] Live in peace with each other.

^{14} *And we urge you, brothers and sisters, [3] warn those who are idle and disruptive,*

[4] encourage the disheartened,

[5] help the weak,

[6] be patient with everyone.

^{15} *[7] Make sure that nobody pays back wrong for wrong,*

but always [8] strive to do what is good for each other and for everyone else.

^{16} *[9] Rejoice always,*

^{17} *[10] pray continually,*

^{18} *[11] give thanks in all circumstances; for this is God's will for you in Christ Jesus.*

^{19} *[12] Do not quench the Spirit.*

^{20} *[13a] Do not treat prophecies with contempt* ^{21} *but [13b] test them all;*

[14] hold on to what is good,

^{22} *[15] reject every kind of evil.*

²³ *May God himself, the God of peace, sanctify you through and through. May your whole spirit, soul and body be kept blameless at the coming of our Lord Jesus Christ.* ²⁴ *The one who calls you is faithful, and he will do it.*

²⁵ *Brothers and sisters, pray for us.* ²⁶ *Greet all God's people with a holy kiss.* ²⁷ *I charge you before the Lord to have this letter read to all the brothers and sisters.*

²⁸ *The grace of our Lord Jesus Christ be with you.*

This short letter seems to have several endings. First, Paul seemed to be wrapping things up at the end of chapter three but didn't. Perhaps someone said, "Hey Paul, what about their questions about the future?" Perhaps he then added answers and thought he'd add some more exhortations after those Q&A sessions. Second, the present ending in chapter five starts and stops and adds and clarifies and then prays and then greets everyone and then, finally, signs off. Sometimes people know it's time to end but stuff just starts bubbling out and before long they need to begin their stopping all over.

We can call this passage "systemic" because Paul goes from top to bottom, inside to outside, and from one side to the other with, count them, fifteen instructions.

ONE AND TWO

He begins with instructions about relationships with one's church leaders. Behind the NIV's "acknowledge" is the word "to know." It's slightly different than acknowledge and suggests knowing, recognizing, understanding, and trusting them. To "acknowledge" [1a in the translation] is tied tightly to [1b] "hold them in highest regard" in verse two, so much so that many think the two are saying one thing with two words: know and esteem together speak of respect and honor. That is, verse one and two are one long sentence. I write this in the roil of failing and falling pastoral leaders, some of whom have committed sexual sins and nearly all have committed sins of authoritarianism. Some will be triggered into more trauma when they hear "acknowledge" and "hold them in the highest regard" (5:12-13). Paul would never pass on blanket endorsement of all leaders in all situations. He knows bad from good leaders.

The terms he uses for leaders begin with "those who work hard" or labor for your spiritual formation. Then he uses a term that means "standing in front" or "leading the way," which the NIV translates into "who care for you in the Lord." Then he turns to "admonish" as one of their tasks, a term that connotes mentoring. The instruction for the Thessalonians is to consider or honor them "uber-abundantly." That fresh coining of a word is because that's what Paul does. He combines "over" with "from" and "abundant." He wants them to show them profuse respect "in love" because of what they do for them. Here we find pastoral leaders who have loving relationships with those in their care and people who love their leaders because they are known to them. Only this relationship makes these words about respect viable.

Paul ends verse thirteen with "Be peaceful among them!" or "Be peaceful among yourselves!" The Greek manuscripts on this one are a toss-up because some should be translated "them" and others "yourselves." Each is true. One ties the instruction to relationship with leaders and the other leads off the long list to follow.

Speaking of a long list, Beverly Gaventa suggests that vv. 12–22 can look like a grocery list (Gaventa, *1–2Thess*,

161

79), and you may think it looks like one too. She clarifies by saying it may look like a random list but there are general topics that keep some of the instructions aimed in the same direction: workers in the community/church (14–15), the discouraged (16–22), and community conduct, perhaps in worship. Byron suggests a different organization: respect leaders (12–13), minister to others (14–15), focus on God (16–18), and keep order in the worship (19–22).

Three to Fifteen

The Christian life is a relational life. It is a mistake to reduce it, however important, to one's personal, private relationship with the Lord. Most of the Christian life instructions in the New Testament are about inter-personal relationships with other humans. Read verses twelve through twenty-two and you will find fifteen imperatives. The first nine are about relationships with one another and only at numbers 10–12 do we see the private relationship with God at work, with numbers 13a and 13b explaining 12 and numbers 14–15 expressing moral obligations given to us by God. It's a kind of Love others, Love God list. How we treat others expresses our relationship with God. I want to recommend a series of four books that beautifully balances our private and our public life. The author is James Bryan Smith and the series is called *The Good and Beautiful Series*. They begin with God, then Life, then Community, and finally You. My reading of spiritual formation books has led me to conclude that too many are exclusively about the Me-and-God approach and not enough about the We-with-One-Another approach. Smith's books balance these wonderfully, as does Paul.

Because the list is long and explanations are on the surface, I will provide my own translation of what remains of these instructions, which reflected the sorts of expectations early believers had for one another. It is not easy to organize this list into topics or audience groups, so I translate it as a list as the letter itself provides no clear arrangement.

14 We encourage you, siblings:
15 See that no one pays back to someone bad with bad, but always chase The Good to one another and to all!
16 Always rejoice!
17 Pray incessantly!
18 Give thanks in everything! For this is God's plan in Christos Yēsous for you.
19 Don't snuff out the Spirit!
20 Don't devalue prophecies!
21 Judge all things suitable!
22 Stay away from evil's every appearance!

What looks a bit random is also common enough for Paul to give a very similar list in Romans 12:3–18. You might read both and create columns to compare the two. It's also a temptation, not one that can be easily avoided, to wonder how many of these instructions actually reflected something going on in the churches in Thessalonica.

A Prayer for Systemic Holiness

What we pray for first often reveals our hearts. Opening up on a note of peace ("the God of peace"; 5:23) raises our eyes up the page to verse thirteen, which either ended instructions about pastoral mentors or began the long list of instructions about the assembly's life. Peace mattered in Thessalonica. This emphasis of God as the peace-God shapes the meaning of "sanctify you," which suggests they need to be top-to-bottom devoted to God and to one another in such a way that peace rules the community's life.

Paul's "through and through" paraphrases very well the Greek term that means completely and holistically, but that's enough for the apostle. He continues with the word "whole," which plays on the previous term (from *holotelēs* to *holoklēros*) to mean "every part" of who you are: "spirit, soul and body" (5:23). The most popular term for this is *systemic*: Paul prays for systemic holiness and devotion to God's will among the Thessalonians. Every item in the list of fifteen instructions is summed up in systemic devotion and blamelessness. He knows the sinful believers will be entirely purged of their sin and dressed up in the beauties and glories of complete devotion to God and to one another in the kingdom of God.

He knows this not because he's some cheery-eyed dreamer but because "the One who calls you is faithful." That One "will do it" (5:24). What God promises, happens; what God wants, occurs. What God promises and wants is for the people of God to be made fit for life with God in the eternal kingdom of God, what the Revelation calls "New Jerusalem."

PASS ON THE GRACE

Many who read Paul's letter skim the final verses, thinking he's done and there's nothing important left. But hold on. John Byron says the formulaic nature of letter endings "becomes the gospel in Paul's hands" (Byron, *1–2Thess*, 203). He continues to end this letter with a request that they pray for him (5:25), and that they pass the greeting of peace to one another by kissing one another's cheeks (5:26), what Paul now calls a "holy kiss," or a holy love-tap.

Paul goes strong next. He says, "I charge you," or "I make you swear before the Lord," "to have this letter read to all the brothers and sisters" (5:27). To begin with, Paul has now picked up the quill to scratch out this and the last verse (Weima, *1–2Thess*, 429). He makes this explicit a few times in his letters (Galatians 6:11; 1 Corinthians 16:21; Philemon 19). Second, Weima says it right when he says the term Paul chooses has a "strident tone" (429). To make them swear that they will do this seems sudden, surprising, and strong. Why? We can only guess, so I will: there must have been sufficient divisions in the house churches that some may have grabbed this letter and hidden it from the others. Can't you see this happening in your church? In particular, the idle or the disorderly members may have been excluded, and Paul wants to make sure they *especially* hear his words.

So he passes on the grace (5:28).

QUESTIONS FOR REFLECTION AND APPLICATION

1. How might Paul's instruction to regard church leaders highly be painful to people who have been harmed by church leaders? How do Paul's further words about those leaders show that Paul is only speaking about respecting good and healthy leaders?

2. There are different ideas on how to organize and group Paul's list of instructions such as shown in Gaventa's and Byron's ideas. How would you organize the list?

3. How should we integrate loving God and loving others? To what extent do our interpersonal relationships impact our relationship with God, and how does our relationship with God affect our relationships with other people?

4. Imagine Paul directing this list of instructions at you. How compliant is your life to this set of goals for a faithful Christian life?

5. As you pursue "systemic" holiness in your life of following Jesus, in what areas do you most want God's help?

FOR FURTHER READING

James Bryan Smith, *The Good and Beautiful God, The Good and Beautiful Life, The Good and Beautiful Community,* and *The Good and Beautiful You* (Downers Grove: IVP, 2009–2022).

GOD'S JUSTICE AND THE POWERLESS

2 Thessalonians 1:1–12

¹ Paul, Silas and Timothy,

To the church of the Thessalonians in God our Father and the Lord Jesus Christ:

² Grace and peace to you from God the Father and the Lord Jesus Christ.

³ We ought always to thank God for you, brothers and sisters, and rightly so, because your faith is growing more and more, and the love all of you have for one another is increasing. ⁴ Therefore, among God's churches we boast about your perseverance and faith in all the persecutions and trials you are enduring.

⁵ All this is evidence that God's judgment is right, and as a result you will be counted worthy of the kingdom of God, for which you are suffering. ⁶ God is just: He will pay back trouble to those who trouble you ⁷ and give relief to you who are troubled, and to us as well. This will happen when the Lord Jesus is revealed from heaven in blazing fire with his powerful angels. ⁸ He will punish those who do not know God and do not obey the gospel of our Lord Jesus. ⁹ They will be punished with everlasting destruction and shut out from the presence of the Lord and from the glory of his might [10] *on the day he comes to be glorified in his holy people and to be marveled at among all those who have believed. This includes you, because you believed our testimony to you.*

[11] *With this in mind, we constantly pray for you, that our God may make you worthy of his calling, and that by his power he may bring to fruition your every desire for goodness and your every deed prompted by faith.* [12] *We pray this so that the name of our Lord Jesus may be glorified in you, and you in him, according to the grace of our God and the Lord Jesus Christ.*

One of the most difficult "encouragements" many of us hear occurs when things are going badly for us. Someone says to us, "Someday God will make it right." You mutter, either to yourself or aloud, "But justice is now." Victims of abuse–power, spiritual, sexual, racial, gender, systemic–want justice. They deserve it. They deserve it now, and we can sometimes make a difference in establishing justice now. However, and I don't like having to use the term "however" though we must at times, there are seasons when those who have experienced injustice are so powerless and so far away from being heard or so excluded from those in power who can establish justice, that the persons have but one option: turning to God in lament, protest, prayer, and hope. The earliest Christians experienced various forms of persecution, though it hadn't yet become anything officially sanctioned by the emperor of Rome. The believers were outnumbered, were rarely citizens, and often so far from those with power that they learned to cope with two strategies: (1) resilient faith and (2) future justice.

THE POWERLESS

As with 1 Thessalonians, this letter has three authors, and "we" and "us" in the letter reveal that all three made contributions to this letter. The three are Paul, Silas, and Timothy (2 Thessalonians 1:1). They write to the Thessalonians in northern Greece. There weren't very many of them; the city was big and filled with the way of Roman power and might. The believers are experiencing opposition to the point of "suffering" (1:5) and "trouble" (1:6), though we don't know the details. It could be social–they lost status. It could be relational– they were more isolated from those who "matter." It could be economic–their networks were broken. It could be physical–they were bruised and beaten and imprisoned. It could be cultural–they no longer "fit" in Thessalonica. We don't know for sure, but something like one or more of these were at work for them.

What to do when no one listens, cares, nor works justice for you?

RESILIENT FAITH

You concentrate on living faithfully, allegiant to the Lord Jesus, and carry on with resilience. That is, you live a resilient faith regardless of your status and conditions.

Resilience begins when you know who you are. They are "the church . . . in God our Father and the Lord Jesus Christ" (1:1) and the three authors pray for God's "grace and peace" for them (1:2). They are God's people, and their true Lord is not the emperor of Rome (Nero probably) but a Galilean artisan Messiah who was crucified by Rome but raised by God and ascended to the right hand of the Father. That's who they are: they are his! They can say this to themselves every morning when they get up.

The authors state they "ought always to thank God" for these believers. They ought to because God has given them grace, they have received that grace, they have acted out that grace by showing it to others, and now Paul witnesses that cycle of grace in them (Brookins, *1–2Thess*, 158). They owe it as a duty to God, and John Byron points us to the common language the church uses in prayer when we pray, and I use the older version of *The Book of Common Prayer* to illustrate the sense of obligation and duty:

> It is very meet, right, and our bounden duty, that we should at all times, and in all places, give thanks unto thee, O Lord, holy Father, almighty, everlasting God.*

Gratitude may be spontaneous but nonetheless is an obligation. Paul sees the resilience of their faith as deserving of honor, which is why they are obligated to give thanks to God and to boast about the Thessalonians (1:4). What the authors are grateful for is that the Thessalonians' faith "is growing more and more" and their "love . . . for one another is increasing" (1:3). That faith and love exhibit themselves in their resilience in "all the persecutions and trials" (1:4). Faith as allegiance and ongoing trust in God and love for other believers take top ranking on Christian virtue lists. But faith and love are both sorely stressed when one is in prison away from one's family, at a loss

---

* https://www.bcponline.org/HE/he1.html

for income and resources to provide for one's family, and when others sneer at them in the marketplace. So for the authors to affirm them–with "growing more and more" and "increasing"–shows to us their firmness of faith, their resilient allegiance, and their intensified growth in commitment to one another.

Instead of scattering, these believers huddled together, locked arms, and said "Together is better." For them church was a refuge, very much like the churches for people of color in our big cities. Instead of scattering, our fellow Americans gather with one another in a common quest for justice inspired by the gospel and the hope of the kingdom. Instead of embracing a theology shaped too much by a white system, they form a black or brown theology shaped by and for their particular situation (Warnock, *The Divided Mind of the Black Church*). Where some of us see personal salvation, they can see holistic redemption and justice; where some of us see in the Gospels Jesus saving a person, they see Jesus breaking down ethnic boundary markers to welcome gentiles to the table. I'm thinking of Matthew 8:5–13 and the centurion's servant. Raphael Warnock, present pastor of the historic Ebenezer Baptist in Atlanta and a U.S. Senator, observes that "the faith of the black church is different from that of the white church," and he's right (Warnock, *The Divided Mind of the Black Church*, 61). My black students and colleagues say the same.

Why bring this up? Here's why: those who are marginalized by the system, as the Thessalonians were, *form a theology, an approach to justice, and a Christian life tailored for their location in the system.* They learn to be resilient, they learn ways to protest that keep them from being imprisoned, they drag their feet when they can, they speak up when they can, they resist as they are able, and they scrum together because only a life together will give them the strength to meet the sun's rising with faith and love. The privileged white suburbanite doesn't form a theology or a Christian life shaped by "resilient faith." Ask yourself what terms are used in your church for the Christian life and ask how much of it is about justice, about resilience for the marginalized, and a gospel that gives empowerment.

FUTURE JUSTICE

The marginalized sing songs called "Spirituals," and they often carry a double message. Their apparent hope of heaven and justice before God had a subtle theme that the future might start now if they could just cross the Ohio River. Their heaven was also code language, at least at times, for what may be tomorrow.

> I look'd over Jordan, an' what did I see
> Comin' for to carry me home,
> A band of angels comin' after me,
> Comin' for to carry me home.

One of the angels in that song was Harriet Tubman, and home was north of the Ohio River (Blount, Thurman).

You may ask, why bring these Spirituals up? Here's why: the future justice theme of 2 Thessalonians 1:5–10[**] is just that: a 1st Century Christian hope for justice that encouraged them to huddle together and plot how to live in a world that seemed against them top to bottom. Their

---

[**] 2 Thessalonians 1:5–10 is one sentence in Greek!

173

hope for future justice brought Amens! and You betchas! from the back row. No one wants justice more than those experiencing injustice, and a desire for justice is not anger but instead righteous indignation for God to put the world into the shape that matches the divine design.

What may be unnoticed is what Paul says in 1:5. He writes, "All this is evidence that God's judgment is right." The evidence is their resilience under pressure that God works in their spiritual formation. Resilience proves God right.

Here's what they believed: (1) God is just (1:6) or, as I would translate, "since it's right [or just] with God to pay back trouble to those who trouble you." If God is just and eventually makes all things right, then it's right for God to undo the injustices they experience. They also believed (2) God would make things right "when the Lord Jesus is revealed from heaven in blazing fire with his powerful angels" (1:7). If God makes things right, injustices must be undone so (3) God "will punish those who do not know God and do not obey the gospel of our Lord Jesus" (1:8). Paul continues in vv. 9–10 to develop God's future justice. (4) Refresh your memory by recalling how many believers were huddling in Thessalonica. Not many. Yet this small band of believers knows full well that someday God will undo all these injustices and they will be the beneficiaries "on the day he comes to be glorified in his holy people" (1:10). God is just, God makes all things right, sin will be eliminated, justice will be established. Instead of getting lost in the weeds of speculations let us concentrate on the big picture: God's work is to make all things right.

We need to take sensitive note of the potential danger

of the fierce language of 1:5–10. Behind some pulpits this language becomes vindictive retribution spoken with glee and *Schadenfreude*–taking pleasure in the misfortune of others. If that is your temptation, skip these verses until you can see them in a better light. These verses are lit up not by vindication but by a desire for justice, which of course involves the erasure of evil and the stopping of systemic sins, but the long-term vision is on the establishment of justice. Desire for a just world drives the language of this passage and should drive us as well. Beverly Gaventa is attentive to the potential misuse of this language and warns us to see that this is concerned with "an angry cry on behalf of a small and beleaguered community which knows God will not leave its suffering without answer" (Gaventa, *1–2Thess*, 105).

SO THEY PRAY

They write "with this in mind" (1:11), "we constantly pray for you." Their daily prayers–morning, afternoon and evening–are God's work in the Thessalonians that God will make them "worthy," which means "deserving" in the sense of God making them qualified for his presence. And they pray that God's "power" will "bring to fruition" the very things they most need: "goodness" and practices "prompted by faith" (1:11). Their prayers are not so the believers will be honored with monuments on street corners but that "the name of our Lord Jesus may be glorified in you" because of God's "grace" at work among them (1:12). Which means this: people will see their resilient faith and their habits of goodness and they will say "those folks look like Jesus."

QUESTIONS FOR REFLECTION AND APPLICATION

1. What types of sufferings were the Thessalonians dealing with?

2. How did they respond to the troubles, and what did that resilience communicate to Paul about their faith?

3. Why is gratitude an obligation for a Christian?

4. What terms does your church use for Christian living? How often do you hear words of justice for the marginalized?

5. In what ways do you feel powerless in your life? How have you experienced injustice? How has this shaped your theology?

FOR FURTHER READING

Blount, "The Negro Spiritual," in *Cultural Interpretation: Reorienting New Testament Criticism* (Minneapolis: Fortress, 1995), 55–69.

Howard Thurman, *Deep River* and *The Negro Spiritual Speaks of Life and Death* (Richmond, Ind.: Friends United Press, 1975)

Raphael G. Warnock, *The Divided Mind of the Black Church: Theology, Piety, and Public Witness* (New York: New York University Press, 2014).

A QUESTION ABOUT WHAT HAPPENS BEFORE THE COMING OF CHRIST

2 Thessalonians 2:1–12

¹ Concerning the coming of our Lord Jesus Christ and our being gathered to him, we ask you, brothers and sisters, ² not to become easily unsettled or alarmed by the teaching allegedly from us—whether by a prophecy or by word of mouth or by letter—asserting that the day of the Lord has already come. ³ Don't let anyone deceive you in any way, for that day will not come until the rebellion occurs and the man of lawlessness is revealed, the man doomed to destruction. ⁴ He will oppose and will exalt himself over everything that is called God or is worshiped, so that he sets himself up in God's temple, proclaiming himself to be God.

⁵ Don't you remember that when I was with you I used to tell you these things? ⁶ And now you know what is holding him back, so that he may be revealed at the proper time. ⁷ For the secret power of lawlessness is already at work; but the one who now holds it back will continue to do so till he is taken out of the way. ⁸ And then the lawless one will be revealed, whom the Lord Jesus will overthrow with the breath of his mouth and destroy by the splendor of his coming. ⁹ The coming of the lawless one will be in accordance with how Satan works. He will use all sorts of displays of power through signs and wonders that serve the lie, ¹⁰ and all the ways that wickedness deceives those who are perishing. They perish because they refused to love the truth and so be saved. ¹¹ For this reason God sends them a powerful delusion so that they will believe the lie ¹² and so that all will be condemned who have not believed the truth but have delighted in wickedness.

In 1 Thessalonians the apostle, along with Silas and Timothy, responded to two questions about the second coming of Christ. One question about those who died before Christ returns (4:13–18) and one about dates and times (5:1–11). Now 2 Thessalonians addresses another of their questions: Has Christ already returned? (2:1–12). Some themes in Christian teachings generate bundles of questions, like heaven and hell and what happens to our loved ones when they die. Questions about Jesus' second coming and when and where and how are among the top-most asked questions. It is then no surprise that Paul addresses such questions in both letters. I speculate that there were a few persons in these house churches who just couldn't get enough information about the second coming. I've been in churches with persons like that, and you might be surprised that some are asking the very question Paul attempts to answer in our passage.

THE QUESTION

Some in Thessalonica believed or, better yet, some had "quickly" (NIV has "easily" in v. 2) shifted away from what they had been taught to think now "that the day of the

Lord had already come." The "day of the Lord" has already been mentioned (1 Thessalonians 5:2; 2 Thessalonians 1:10). That day includes two ideas–the return of Christ and the judgment of God against sin. Since it would have been very obvious to them that this had not happened physically, those with the question must have thought the return of Christ was a spiritual event that had already occurred. I have met people alive today who believe the return of Christ occurred in 70 AD or some other date or that, instead, it was entirely spiritual anyway. Here the emphasis is on "the coming of our Lord Jesus Christ and our being gathered to him" (2:1). Which means some think Jesus made a secret return and left behind those who are in Thessalonica. So the essence of the problem was that some claimed Jesus had already returned.

The problem thickens. Those asking this question seem to have claimed Paul himself taught this very thing. Paul does not seem sure whether they had gotten whiff of this. Was it "by a prophecy or by word of mouth or by letter" (2:2)? Paul never communicated such a thing so he makes it clear that it is "allegedly from us" (2:2). Paul's opponents are making things up about his teachings. In our day false teachers often claim their teachings are biblical, and sometimes they have received their special insider teachings in an ecstatic trance or in a vision or they heard it in a prophetic utterance.

PASTORAL RESPONSES

There is a tendency for some to erupt into loud language and fierce threats when they hear someone teaching bad ideas in their church or circles. And sometimes it is about topics that are neither heretical nor dangerous, even if they are beliefs the pastor or some concerned leader does not teach or believe. The great thinkers in the history of the church have learned to think from the center out. That is, to begin with the gospel about Jesus (1 Corinthians 15:1–28) and ask if some new teaching denies that gospel. Then to think about the fundamental conclusions of the church as found in the Nicene Creed (see https://www.creeds.net/ancient/nicene.htm).

Does what is being taught deny any line in the Creed? Only then do we go to our special statements of faith, that is, the specific teachings of our local church or our denomination. Often what is causing concerns is some minor issue–someone is pre-trib and another person believes in a post-trib rapture. (Yes, that's a minor issue except to the person who thinks it's a major issue, which it is not.)

Paul's response is not a heated reaction, though at times he can let it fly. Instead, he offers warm, pastorally sensitive wisdom. Paul offers words of assurance when, instead of not demanding, he requests for them "not to become easily unsettled or alarmed" (2:2). He wants them to trust the truth of what they have learned and not to be deceived (2:3). After assuring them he reminds them that he had taught about this to them when he was present (2:5) and they thus already "know" the truth (2:6).

I can't resist observing that *lots is lost* in teaching people. Apart from either standing on your head or some other dramatically unforgettable approach, or apart from going over something many times with lots of question and response time, somewhere between some to almost all of what we teach will be forgotten. One of my own students reads each of these studies and then writes the questions. Her name is Becky and I asked her what she remembers of what I taught in classes. She responded by saying "maybe

40% of the big ideas (the main repeated concepts, themes, advice, and rules) and 10% of the specific details . . . good thing I took notebook upon notebook of notes and kept all the class handouts! (But one thing I remember for sure, from the repetition in every Gospels class: the Jesus Creed. I say it every morning when I first wake up.)"

So, having taught, it did not sink in as deeply as Paul had hoped. Which is why he offers the pastorally sensitive words.

His pastoral approach now turns to specific instructions about his previous instructions regarding the return of Christ.

First These

He reminds them that before "the coming of our Lord Jesus Christ and our being gathered to him" first these events must occur:

1. The Rebellion (2:3), or Apostasy.
2. The Man of Lawlessness is revealed (2:3).
3. That man will oppose God and exalt himself above God (2:4).
4. That man will "set himself up in God's temple" (2:4).
5. That man will declare "himself to be God" (2:4).
6. That man will be in union with Satan and will perform acts of power, deceiving many with The Lie (2:9–12).
7. Something is presently holding him back until God's time (2:7–8).
8. The Lord Jesus will judge that man and those allegiant to him (2:8, 10–12).

We can't be sure now where Paul got all this information, but much of it, if not nearly all of it, shows up in Jesus' predictions in the Gospels (esp. Mark 13) and in the Book of Revelation, with echoes in Daniel and Isaiah. It is not speculative to see these specific items in his teachings as standard fare in early Christian teachings about the future.

Still speculations will arise immediately when some read passages like this. Just try reading this passage in a small group or Bible study and ask folks what they think the passage is teaching. (Maybe you better not.) Here's one of the more bizarre ones I've ever read. Change "beast" in this passage to "Man of Lawlessness" and it all falls into the same network of nonsense:

> Since Trump's election in November of 2016, many have linked him to the beast of Revelation and the number 666, noting, among other portents, that his election year, 2016, is the sum of 666 + 666 + 666 + 6 +6 + 6; that he frequently makes an "okay" sign that forms the number six; and that his son-in-law Jared Kushner's real estate company owns 666 Fifth Avenue in New York. (Timothy Beal's *The Book of Revelation: A Biography*, 202)

Seriously. One of the questions we might ask is, "Who in the world figures this kind of stuff out?"

Instead of getting lost in speculations like these, and misreading the texts of the Bible, here's a big picture summary of what Paul wrote in 2 Thessalonians 2: in the future the so-called "Man of Lawlessness" will appear on the world's scene when evil will seem to seize control of the world's systems. Paul does not seem to have heard of someone called "The Antichrist," but his Man fits the

Antichrist images we learn in other parts of the Bible. This label points to a person who is reckless, anarchist, and against the revealed will of God. He defiles what is holy and sacred by entering the temple and declaring that he is God, and this almost certainly sends everyone's mind in Thessalonica to Rome and the claims of emperors to be divine or sons of the divine. Which means they all shifted to think of a Roman emperor, not unlike Caesar Augustus or Nero. Like the dark figures of Revelation, miracles are done by these shadowy figures, not by the power of God but through the power of the Adversary, Satan, and all of this combines into what Paul here calls "The Lie."

The most difficult expression in our chapter is "the one who now holds it back will continue to do so till he is taken out of the way" (2:7). Sometimes "it" is referred to as "The Restrainer." This person, if it is a person, could be (1) God or the Spirit of God, the archangel Michael, or Paul himself; (2) it could be governmental powers that have enough justice to prevent a spiral into systemic evil, and for Paul that would probably be Rome; (3) or it could be Satan holding back to unleash the "Man of Lawlessness" until God permits or until the time is ripe for Satan to go into full attack mode. Recent studies favor the Restrainer being Michael, and one can see more about him by reading Daniel 10–12, esp. 10:13–14 and 11:36–37 (Gupta, 1–2Thess, 250–257). But let's remind ourselves: do we really know this with confidence? (No.)

Let's not get lost in the weeds of speculating Who and When. We need to keep the big picture in mind, and once Tom Wright put that big picture like this:

One day all creation will be rescued from slavery, from the corruption, decay, and death which deface its beauty, destroy its relationships, remove the sense of God's presence from it, and make it a place of injustice, violence, and brutality (Wright, *Simply Christian*, 126).

Many of the church's leaders have admitted in humility that they are not sure what Paul was on about here, that is, when it comes to specifics. Instead, we can allow our minds to concentrate, beside the big picture just quoted, on these two central ideas:

(1) Jesus has not returned yet because these things have not yet occurred, and (2) evil is real, and it has the capacity at some point to overcome the world in a death grip that will only be snapped by God.

For Paul that kind of evil has not yet occurred either. So, there is no need to believe these false reports about what Paul was teaching. Instead, carry on with faithful living and gospel mission. A danger the Thessalonians were facing was false teaching, deceptive doctrines, and intoxicating falsehoods. Beverly Gaventa is right in summarizing this passage as the "Defeat of Delusion" (Gaventa, *1–2Thess*, 107).

QUESTIONS FOR REFLECTION AND APPLICATION

1. How does Paul pastorally approach reassuring people when they have troubling questions?

2. In your Christian experience, have you personally been troubled about understanding the End Times, or have you seen others consumed by these questions? How has that manifested itself?

3. What big ideas can help us make sense of the details of End Times passages such as this one?

4. Who would you consider "false teachers" in the church today? How do their teachings oppose the gospel and the creeds of the church?

5. How much do you remember from the teachings of the influential Christian leaders in your life? What are some of the key messages and lessons that stand out to you, and what made them stick for you?

FOR FURTHER READING

Timothy Beal, *The Book of Revelation: A Biography* (Princeton: Princeton University Press, 2018).
N.T. Wright, *Simply Christian: Why Christianity Makes Sense* (New York: HarperOne, 2010).

GIFTS AND OBLIGATIONS

2 Thessalonians 2:13–17

13 But we ought always to thank God for you, brothers and sisters loved by the Lord, because God chose you as firstfruits to be saved through the sanctifying work of the Spirit and through belief in the truth. 14 He called you to this through our gospel, that you might share in the glory of our Lord Jesus Christ.

15 So then, brothers and sisters, stand firm and hold fast to the teachings we passed on to you, whether by word of mouth or by letter.

16 May our Lord Jesus Christ himself and God our Father, who loved us and by his grace gave us eternal encouragement and good hope, 17 encourage your hearts and strengthen you in every good deed and word.

Grace, which is a gift from God to a person, has the power not only to redeem a person and a community but to form a relationship, or a social bond, between God and people. A relationship with God has the capacity to transform us into people of gratitude, of faithfulness, and of hope. There is a back-and-forthness about gift-giving, or grace, that illuminates how God's grace to us works.

A contemporary philosopher to Paul, in the inner circle of the emperor, Seneca, wrote a whole book about gifts called *On Benefits*. He illustrates the relationship of a giver and receiver with two persons playing catch with a ball. Gift-giving in Paul's world was like playing a game of catch. One tossed the ball, another caught it, and the one catching it tossed it back. One isn't playing catch if one simply catches and holds on to the ball. I quote from Seneca, and it is worth your time (and fun) to read this excerpt carefully. Remember, he's illustrating the back-and-forth relationship of a giver and receiver of a gift, and this back-and-forthness will help us understand God's grace to us. Seneca writes,

> I would like to use the example of ball playing advanced by the Stoic Chrysippus. There is no doubt that when the ball is dropped it could be the fault of either the thrower or the catcher. The game goes along nicely when the ball is thrown and caught by both in a suitable manner, back and forth between the hands of thrower and catcher. But a good player needs to throw the ball differently to a tall partner and to a short one.

It is the same with gift-giving: unless it is adjusted to the social roles of both parties, the giver and the recipient, the gift will not actually be given by the one nor be received by the other in the right manner.

If we are dealing with an experienced player who is in good condition, we will throw the ball more adventurously, knowing that however it comes at him his quick and nimble hand will knock it back. If we are playing with an untrained novice, however, we will not send it to him in such a firm and percussive manner, but more gently, and we will just barely meet it when it's volleyed back to us, guiding it right into his hand.

> We should do the same with gift-giving (slightly adjusted translation; 2:17.3–4).

Notice another dimension of gift-giving in the ancient world: there is obligation to respond. You don't just hang on to the ball tossed to you.

Someone who merely accepts a gift, no matter how good his attitude is, has not yet fulfilled his obligation. For there is still an aspect of repayment left. It is just as in a game: it is one thing to catch the ball with skill and care, but you cannot be called a good player unless you are quick and nimble in returning the ball you have caught (32.1).

This sense of gift-giving with obligation to respond appropriately shapes so much of Paul's theology but especially we see the sense of obligation in 2 Thessalonians.

OBLIGATION OF GRACE

Paul repeats in nearly identical language what he said in 1:3 when 2:13 opens with "we *ought* always to thank God." This sense of obligation, again, ushers us into a set of ideas that begin with God's grace and gift in his Son, of the gift of redemption, of the Thessalonians experiencing that redemption and tossing back the gift with thanksgiving, and with Paul observing it all as one who feels a sense of similar duty of giving thanks for them because of what God has done (Barclay, *Paul and the Gift*).

Grace and obligation are not opposites but partners

in the experience of grace. What Paul is obligated to God the Father for is that, in God's gift-giving, they are "loved by the Lord [Jesus]" and that "God [the Father] chose," or "lifted them out of their idolatries" (2:13). God did this so they could be like other gentile believers in Jesus, the "first fruits" of salvation, a redemption that he depicts as God transforming them into a life of dedication to God "through the sanctifying work of the Spirit" (2:13). Yes, the passage carries the tone of the Trinity as Father, Son, and Spirit are each mentioned in distinction to One Another. This God "called" them "through the gospel" so they could "share in the glory of our Lord Jesus Christ" (2:14), another indicator of the return of Christ and their gathering to him to be with him forever in the kingdom (2:1–12).

The Thessalonians were drawn into redemption by God's Spirit; Paul witnessed it all, and now Paul is obligated to return that divine toss back to God in thanksgiving as they await the second coming. His theology and writing here are beautiful, and they remind me of something in Dorothy Sayers' wonderful novel, *Gaudy Night*. Here's what she wrote about writing:

> "Isn't the writing of good prose an emotional excitement?"
>
> "Yes, of course it is. At least, when you get the thing dead right and know it's dead right, there's no excitement like it. It's marvellous. It makes you feel like God on the Seventh Day—for a bit, anyhow."

The flourishing words and splendid romp through how grace works makes me wonder if Paul didn't throw his hands behind his head, say a word of thanks, and then say, "Wow, what a wonderful way of thinking about God's love for us."

OBLIGATION OF INSTRUCTION

Their obligation to God is "stand firm and hold fast" to what was taught in "Sunday School" classes, in catechism, and in discipleship letters they had sent them. Call it what you like. Paul had taught them about the return of Christ, and they had become unsettled about it (2:2). He wants them to hang on to that earlier teaching as the truth about the future. His images for his instructions evoke strong responses:

> *Plant your feet* so you can resist the blows and blocks;
> *grip tightly* the apostolic teachings, the truth of
> the gospel.

Their redemption prompts obligation to that teaching.

Failing to Grip Scripture Tightly

1. Taking verses out of context
2. Adhering to unbiblical views
3. Permitting popular teachers and authors to have more weight
4. Uncritically accepting "prophetic utterances"
5. Emphasizing one part of Scripture over others
6. Using a new interpretation of a passage to overturn other clearer ones

7. Believing what you prefer rather than what Scripture says
8. Suggesting Scripture is no longer relevant

From Michael Holmes, *1–2Thess*, 265–266

OBLIGATION OF ENCOURAGEMENT

The reciprocating circle, the back-and-forthness, continues: God gives grace, they receive the gift, they return the gift with thankful faithfulness–and now he prays the Gift himself, Jesus, and the Father of the Gift, who in "love" gifted to them "eternal encouragement and good hope," will "encourage" them–and he ends all this with "in grace." It's all grace, it's all gift, and God's gifting transforms the receivers into thank-ers and gift-givers who can be confident they will not experience the "hair-raising" (Holmes, *1–2Thess*, 262) judgments just detailed (2:1–12,16–17). The terms "eternal" and "hope" both evoke again their need to anchor themselves in the previous instructions about the return of Christ.

To cap this short passage off, a reminder: we have a tendency to think of grace as a "pure" or simple gift. That is, it is entirely something God gives to us that we don't deserve. Yes, that's true, but stopping grace as no more than pure gift short cuts what grace and gift-giving meant. Gifts given formed their receivers into relationships that transformed persons into becoming givers themselves.

Let's play catch with God!

QUESTIONS FOR REFLECTION AND APPLICATION

1. What kinds of bonds does grace create?

2. How does Seneca's illustration of gift-giving with a game of catch impact how you view gifts/grace in Scripture?

3. How do grace and obligation work together?

4. What is the back-and-forthness of grace, God's gifts?

5. How has God's grace worked in your life to improve your relationships with God and people?

FOR FURTHER READING

John Barclay, *Paul and the Gift* (Grand Rapids: Wm. B. Eerdmans, 2015).

Dorothy Sayers, *Gaudy Night* (New York: Harper & Row, 1964), 180.

PRAYERS IN ALL DIRECTIONS

2 Thessalonians 3:1–5

[1] As for other matters, brothers and sisters, pray for us that the message of the Lord may spread rapidly and be honored, just as it was with you. [2] And pray that we may be delivered from wicked and evil people, for not everyone has faith. [3] But the Lord is faithful, and he will strengthen you and protect you from the evil one. [4] We have confidence in the Lord that you are doing and will continue to do the things we command. [5] May the Lord direct your hearts into God's love and Christ's perseverance.

Mutual prayers for one another mark the common life of Christians. When one shares, others are prompted to share. Kris and I breakfast one day a week at our local favorite, Anam Cara Café. Kris orders the "Breakfast Plate," and I order the "Breakfast Burrito." Kris shares with me some of her potato squares, and I share with her half of the burrito, which she has for lunch that day or the next day. Sharing prompts sharing. Praying does the same. As Michael W. Smith once sang/wrote, in his song "Pray for Me," "Pray for me, and I'll pray for you."

Pray for Me . . .

Paul often ended his letters with prayer for others but sometimes he asked them to pray for him. He wants them to pray, as Jesus once prayed (Matthew 9:35–38), for expansiveness in gospel preaching (1 Thessalonians 3:1), that is, "that the message of [or "word about"] the Lord may spread rapidly and be honored." Actually his words are more zesty than the NIV's. Thus: "Pray for us that the Lord's word may run ahead and win the glory!" (see Brookins, *1–2Thess*, 185). He wants gospel growth in Corinth to be like the gospel growth in Thessalonica.

But he continues with another request—"that we may be delivered from wicked and evil people"—which reminds us of two other prayer requests by Paul to other churches:

> I urge you, brothers and sisters, by our Lord Jesus Christ and by the love of the Spirit, to join me in my struggle by praying to God for me. *Pray that I may be kept safe from the unbelievers in Judea . . .* (Romans 15:30–31).
>
> I know that through your prayers and God's provision of the Spirit of Jesus Christ what has happened to me *will turn out for my deliverance* (Philippians 1:19).

What connects these verses to one another is that Paul is asking them to pray that he will be protected and his life preserved so he can continue in his gospel work. He knows some oppose the gospel work enough that he calls them over-the-top or out-of-control persons as well as "evil people" (3:2). He probably has some specific group in Corinth in mind, and they are unbelievers ("not everyone has [the] faith").

Paul knew he was as dependent on God as they were, so he asked them to pray for him. Their relationship is siblings, not master-teacher or even apostle-apprentices. Inside all categories of relationships, they were brothers and sisters relating to one another as equals.

. . . AND I WILL PRAY FOR YOU

Prayer turns Paul to God and when he turns to God, he ponders that God is "faithful" and that God will give them "strength" and protection "from the evil one" (3:3). Opposition to the gospel, which Paul experienced everywhere he went (cf. Acts 18:5–17), emerges from the powers of darkness opposed to the power of the light.

Yes, some gaslight others and spiritually abuse others and pull out the evil-one-card and toss it down on the table, saying about some criticism, "This comes from Satan." It takes discerning minds to perceive when this is gaslighting and when it is true spiritual discernment. A clue is given by how often said player-of-the-card responds in humility to discerning criticisms. The standard trick for power abusers is to discredit the critics (when the criticisms aren't discreditable), but when that doesn't work an abuser will resort to demonizing the critics. They may then spin the story into an alternative narrative, gaslight those bringing forth allegations, and when that doesn't work, the abuser will turn the whole thing upside down to make himself (or herself) into the victim of malicious attacks (McKnight-Barringer, *A Church Called Tov*, 55–70). No, I don't think Paul is doing any of these things, but I know many use Paul's words here to do the very things I have just described.

Lord have mercy. Christ have mercy. Lord have mercy.

In his prayer for God's empowering presence among them he puts back on his head the pastor's hat and says, "We have confidence," and one expects *in you* but instead we get "in the Lord" (3:4), which tips his cap toward God's work among them. Pastoral confidence matters to people. Eugene Peterson, in a collection of his sermons, once said this to his congregation (Peterson, *As Kingfishers Catch Fire*, 119):

> Every Sunday I look across this congregation and wonder, prayerfully, what is going on. I know most of you pretty well. But there is a lot I don't know. I am here every week with the conviction that this place of worship is the most important place you can be right now, that the scriptures, hymns, prayers, and sermon can enter into your souls, your lives, bringing you into a deeper participation in eternal life.

That's pastoral care for people, and it puts legs and arms on what Paul meant when he said "we have confidence" about you.

Paul wants them to pray for his mission work and for protection, but he prays that they will continue to be faithful in following out their instructions (again, "our" not "my"), in being guided by the Lord Jesus into "God's love" or "love for God," as well a faith that is nothing less than Christ-resilience (NIV: "Christ's perseverance"; 3:5). Some, to be sure, care only about success and numbers, but Paul's goal is not just to get people saved but to get saved people transformed into loving people. May that be our prayer and mission.

QUESTIONS FOR REFLECTION AND APPLICATION

1. What does Paul ask the people to pray for him? What can you learn from his prayer requests?

2. How does Paul then turn around and encourage them, perhaps indicating that these are the very things he has prayed for them?

3. Have you seen Christians use words like "wicked" and "evil" to demonize victims instead of abusers? How does this lesson help you make sense of such instances?

4. What is the best experience of pastoral care you have ever had with a pastor?

5. If you could reach out to a loving group of Christian friends right now, what would you ask them to pray for you?

FOR FURTHER READING

Scot McKnight, Laura Barringer, *A Church Called Tov* (Carol Stream, Illinois: Tyndale Momentum, 2020).

Eugene Peterson, *As Kingfishers Catch Fire* (Colorado Springs: WaterBrook, 2017).

Michael W. Smith, "Pray for Me," *i 2 Eye* (Reunion, 1988).

WARNING
FREELOADERS

2 Thessalonians 3:6–18

⁶ In the name of the Lord Jesus Christ, we command you, brothers and sisters, to keep away from every believer who is idle and disruptive and does not live according to the teaching you received from us. ⁷ For you yourselves know how you ought to follow our example. We were not idle when we were with you, ⁸ nor did we eat anyone's food without paying for it. On the contrary, we worked night and day, laboring and toiling so that we would not be a burden to any of you. ⁹ We did this, not because we do not have the right to such help, but in order to offer ourselves as a model for you to imitate. ¹⁰ For even when we were with you, we gave you this rule: "The one who is unwilling to work shall not eat."

¹¹ We hear that some among you are idle and disruptive. They are not busy; they are busybodies. ¹² Such people we command and urge in the Lord Jesus Christ to settle down and earn the food they eat. ¹³ And as for you, brothers and sisters, never tire of doing what is good.

¹⁴ Take special note of anyone who does not obey our instruction in this letter. Do not associate with them, in order that they may feel ashamed. [15] *Yet do not regard them as an enemy, but warn them as you would a fellow believer.*

[16] *Now may the Lord of peace himself give you peace at all times and in every way. The Lord be with all of you.*

[17] *I, Paul, write this greeting in my own hand, which is the distinguishing mark in all my letters. This is how I write.*

[18] *The grace of our Lord Jesus Christ be with you all.*

When in the heart of your beliefs and behaviors beats the grace of hospitality, or when the posture of sharing and giving forms your community's way of life, someone will take advantage of your hospitality and giving. Years later than this passage the apostle Paul will warn some young widows about taking advantage of Christian generosity (1 Timothy 5:11–15). In the NIV we have "busybody" and "idle" in both letters (cf. 2 Thessalonians 3:6–7, 11). It should be observed that Paul appears to be warning men in Thessalonica while he warns women in 1 Timothy. Since the term in 3:6 is *adelphos*, which means brother (the NIV has "believer") and the terms use the masculine gender in "some who are idle and disruptive" at 3:11, his warnings in 2 Thessalonians are most likely for specific men. So, the situation appears to be men who are avoiding work by presuming upon hospitality. They are freeloaders, moochers, sponges.

We offer a quick but sometimes needed reminder. These words are not directed at the unintentionally unemployed nor at the underpaid and overwhelmed. No, in view are those who *can* work but who *choose not to* work and then presume upon Christian generosity.

Talk to most employers today and they will soon point

to a glaring issue at work: employees who spend far too much of their time on social media while paid for work. Not working, they are paid for working, which is not that far from the freeloaders in Thessalonica.

WARNING ABOUT FREELOADERS

Freeloading was a problem in the mission churches, not only for mooching, and not only because they weren't adulting well, but also because such behaviors spoiled the reputation of Christ and the church. He describes these people with one word: *ataktōs*. A term that points at those who operate outside the orders of life or those who are order-less in life. The NIV uses two terms to get it right: "idle and disruptive." The term was used at times for soldiers who–I'm thinking of Bill Murray's troop in its "Razzle Dazzle" routine in *Stripes*–wouldn't follow marching orders or who were flouting marching's orderly ways.

In the second paragraph he adds a new term for them. I translate 3:11: "For we hear some are walking around among you in a disorderly manner–not working but working around working." The NIV's "busy" and "busybodies" transfers it all into our lingo, but the activity Paul has in mind is about those who worked at not having to work, or somehow *working around working*, that is, managing to get food without earning it or working for it. These razzle dazzle guys had presumed on some sense of entitlement. The order-less in Thessalonica wanted life to be all play, no work.

We don't know why they were not working, but perhaps they thought Jesus' return was so soon and imminent they were willing to forego work. An imminent return and not working are not connected in this letter, but they are in 1 Thessalonians 4:11–12 and 5:13–14, both of which passages are close to a passage about the Second Coming. Back to 2 Thessalonians. Perhaps they wanted to be full-time evangelists or thought they too deserved the right to support. Or maybe they were lazy. We don't know. I'll leave it with various options.

One more term may just put it all into view. At the end of verse thirteen Paul says "never tire of doing what is good," but the word "good" suggests "excellence." What the moochers were doing was ugly while Paul and his co-workers were displaying one of life's excellencies in working with their hands. The terms "idle and disruptive" summarize the behaviors of not paying for one's food (3:6), not working one's job (3:8, 10), and of not earning one's own food (3:12). They were socially out of order, and their out-of-order-ness worked because everybody else was in order.

RESPONSIBILITY WITH GENEROSITY

Early Christian emphases were personal responsibility, sufficient ambition to work hard enough to provide for one's family, and the discipline to stick to the task. Yes, there was also a net to catch the need called Christian generosity. But such acts of generosity were what today is called "subsidiarity" (see *Compendium*, 104–107). Paul expresses it as "The one who is unwilling to work shall not eat" (3:10). Here is the early Christian sense of generosity and subsidiarity: work with your own hands and for those who can't make ends meet, so there will be a web of benevolence.

A Christian tradition about responsibility and generosity had already formed in the mission churches. Paul says these freeloaders are not living "according to the tradition [NIV: "teaching"] you received from us" (3:6). They learned this "when we were with you" (3:10). The apostle Peter had a big emphasis on the importance of a public life being respectable enough that Christians avoided getting themselves in trouble (1 Peter 2:11–3:22). Christians learned quickly that their powerlessness meant living a good life that would not draw the attention of the authorities against them. Working with one's hands in a responsible life was an early Christian teaching, and it was shaped in part to keep them all out of trouble.

Once again, Paul appeals to the work ethic of himself and his co-workers as an example to follow: "we worked day and night, laboring and toiling" to avoid presuming upon generosity and becoming a burden to his mission churches, and they worked hard "to offer ourselves as a model for you to imitate" (3:8–10). Their work was mostly likely turning cloth or leather into marketable items, and this work was done in a shop that Paul turned into a little classroom or public pulpit (Hock, *The Social Context of Paul's Ministry*). It was hard work; it was hot and sweaty and full of that special intense odor; Paul had strong arms and calloused hands. He acquired sufficient funds to provide food and shelter for himself, Silas, Timothy, and probably more besides. Noticeably, they had "the right to such help" (or the "authority" for support; 3:9).

Social Distancing for a Purpose

Paul tells the Thessalonians to put some social distance between themselves and the social sponges. His words are stiff: "Do not associate," or intermingle, "with them" (3:14). This is not shunning as vindictiveness or even some claim to superiority but instead it is to toss some temporary shade on them that rebukes and communicates disrespect and disappointment for their loafing. The intent is to draw them back into the community as responsible workers who don't take advantage of the generosity of Christian hospitality. He makes the intent clear when he says, "Yet do not regard them as an enemy" (3:15), that is, don't demonize them or turn them into some stereotype of evil. Instead, treat the person as a sibling in Christ and mentor them into a responsible life.

Be careful. In our world, such a person will most likely leave your community life and go to another church where he can take advantage of their generosity. It is wiser in our context to give all the more attention to regular pastoral care and meeting with such a person than to exclude them from the fellowship completely.

SIGNING OFF

Paul finishes off this letter in a customary way: a prayer for peace, his own signature when he takes up the pen himself, and a wish for God's grace (3:16–18). Peace is his prayer, which pertains to relational peace with God, with one's self, with one's family, with one's fellowship, and with one's neighbors in one's community. Peace is that wide. Peace attends those when the "Lord [is] with all" (3:16). God's presence is a big theme in the Bible: think of the pillar of fire in the wilderness, of God's glory in the tabernacle and temple, of the Lord Jesus as "God with us" (Matt 1:23), Immanuel, and think too of the Holy Spirit with us and in the New Jerusalem of God dwelling with the people of God. To prayer-wish God's presence with them launches a life now that looks back to God's presence and forward to God's final endless presence.

Paul's handwriting, like Dietrich Bonhoeffer's and not a few of my students', either was illegible or looked like he never got on to cursive in penmanship. I once had a colleague whose handwriting was accurately called hen scratches.

He signs off with a prayer-wish for grace, which takes us not only back to the beginning of both of the letters to the Thessalonians but also to Philippians—and all the way back for Paul to what happened on the road to Damascus. The biography of Brennan Manning is called *All is Grace*. Paul, Silas, and Timothy all say, "Amen!"

QUESTIONS FOR REFLECTION AND APPLICATION

1. How does Paul's personal example of hard work contrast with the freeloaders he is criticizing here?

2. How is the Christian system of benevolence intended to work?

3. What model does Paul give here of sternly yet gently correcting errant siblings?

4. Have your generosity and hospitality ever been taken advantage of? What was that experience like for you?

5. What is your biggest takeaway from this Bible study volume? What grace has God given you through your diligent study?

FOR FURTHER READING

Ronald Hock, *The Social Context of Paul's Ministry: Tentmaking and Apostleship* (Minneapolis: Fortress, 2007).

Brennan Manning, John Blase, *All is Grace: A Ragamuffin Memoir* (Colorado Springs: David C. Cook, 2011).

On Subsidiarity, see https://en.wikipedia.org/wiki /Subsidiarity_(Catholicism), but especially Compendium of the Social Doctrine of the Church (New York: Continuum International, 2006). Available online at: s/justpeace /documents/rc_pc_justpeace_doc_20060526 _compendio-dott-soc_en.html

New Testament Everyday Bible Study Series

In the **New Testament Everyday Bible Study Series,** widely respected biblical scholar Scot McKnight combines interpretive insights with pastoral wisdom for all the books of the New Testament.

Each volume provides:

- Original Meaning. Brief, precise expositions of the biblical text and offers a clear focus for the central message of each passage.

- Fresh Interpretation. Brings the passage alive with fresh images and what it means to follow King Jesus.

- Practical Application. Biblical connections and questions for reflection and application for each passage.

— AVAILABLE IN THE SERIES —

James and Galatians

Acts

Philippians and 1 & 2 Thessalonians

HarperChristian Resources

The Blue Parakeet

Rethinking How You Read the
Bible

Scot McKnight, author of
The Jesus Creed

Why Can't I Just Be a Christian?

Parakeets make delightful pets. We cage
them or clip their wings to keep them where we
want them. Scot McKnight contends that many, conservatives and lib-
erals alike, attempt the same thing with the Bible. We all try to tame it.

McKnight's *The Blue Parakeet* has emerged at the perfect time to
cool the flames of a world on fire with contention and controversy.
It calls Christians to a way to read the Bible that leads beyond old
debates and denominational battles. It calls Christians to stop taming
the Bible and to let it speak anew for a new generation.

In his books *The Jesus Creed* and *Embracing Grace*, Scot McKnight
established himself as one of America's finest Christian thinkers, an
author to be reckoned with.

In *The Blue Parakeet*, McKnight again touches the hearts and minds
of today's Christians, this time challenging them to rethink how to read
the Bible, not just to puzzle it together into some systematic theology
but to see it as a Story that we're summoned to enter and to carry
forward in our day.

In his own inimitable style, McKnight sets traditional and liberal
Christianity on its ear, leaving readers equipped, encouraged, and em-
boldened to be the people of faith they long to be.

Available in stores and online!

ZONDERVAN

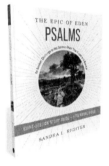
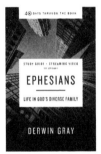
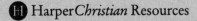

ALSO AVAILABLE FROM
SCOT MCKNIGHT

How to Know, Read, Live, and Show the Gospel

We want to follow King Jesus, but do we know how?

Author and professor Scot McKnight will help you discover what it means to follow King Jesus through 24 lessons based on four of his writings (The King Jesus Gospel, The Blue Parakeet – 2nd edition, One.Life, and A Fellowship of Differents). McKnight's unique framework for discipleship is designed to be used for personal study and within disciple-making groups of two or more. In this workbook, McKnight will help you:

Study Guide
9780310105992

- Know the biblical meaning of the gospel
- Read the Bible and understand how to apply it today
- Live as disciples of Jesus in all areas of life
- Show the world God's character through life together in the church

Each lesson, created by Becky Castle Miller, has both Personal Study and Group Discussion sections. The Personal Study section contains a discipleship reading from Scot McKnight, an insightful Bible study, an insightful Bible study, and a time for individual prayer, action, and reflection. The Group Discussion section includes discussion questions and activities to do together with a discipleship group. You'll share insights from your personal study time with each other and explore different ways of living out what you're learning.

Whether you have been a Christian for many years or you are desiring a fresh look at what it means to be a disciple, this workbook is an in-depth guide to what it means to follow King Jesus and to discover how to put that kind of life into practice.